ACTING
TECHNIQUES
AN INTRODUCTION FOR ASPIRING ACTORS

MICHAEL POWELL

ACTING
TECHNIQUES
AN INTRODUCTION FOR ASPIRING ACTORS

MICHAEL POWELL

methuen | drama

A QUINTET BOOK
Copyright © 2010 Quintet Publishing Limited.

This edition published by
Methuen Drama
A & C Black Publishers Ltd
36 Soho Square
London W1D 3QY
www.methuendrama.com

ISBN: 978 1 408 12734 6

QTT.ACTB

Conceived, designed and produced by
Quintet Publishing Limited
The Old Brewery
6 Blundell Street
London N7 9BH

Project Editor: Martha Burley
Editorial Assistant: Holly Willsher
Consultant: Tony Bell
Designer: Emma Wicks
Copy Editor: Nikky Twyman
Illustrator: Claire Scully
Art Editor: Zoë White
Art Director: Michael Charles
Managing Editor: Donna Gregory
Publisher: James Tavendale

1 3 5 7 9 10 8 6 4 2

Printed in China by 1010 Printing International Limited

DEDICATED TO
THE RADA CLASS
OF '91.

CONTENTS

INTRODUCTION

You can't learn to be a great actor from a book, just as you can't teach yourself to dance, swim, do martial arts, paint, fish, tightrope-walk or climb Everest. Acting is observing and doing. Nevertheless, starting from this flawed premise, this book is intended as a comprehensive introduction to the craft and business of acting for the working actor, drama student or anyone considering a career on stage and screen. It offers an honest account of the vocation, art and business of acting and a foretaste of the challenges you will face both creatively and professionally. The first eight chapters examine acting technique, while the last three focus on the reality of the profession and the business side of marketing yourself, staying on top of things and maintaining your skills and sanity in a highly competitive and overcrowded marketplace.

Observation is a key aspect of the craft and will help you become a better actor.

PENN IN ACTION

SEAN PENN TALKS TO DIRECTOR SYDNEY POLLACK ON SET FOR THE MOVIE *THE INTERPRETER*, 2005
Penn is famous for his dynamic and risk-taking performances. His commitment and visible passion about his work have contributed to his colourful career.

WE ALL PRETEND

If you want to know what it is to be an actor, watch Marlon Brando's famous last interview with Larry King. Brando called acting 'the least mysterious of all crafts. Whenever we want something from somebody or when we want to hide something or pretend, we're acting. Most people do it all day long.' He understood acting both as craft and business and had no illusions about its monumental rewards and titanic pitfalls; his self-knowledge and ennui are almost visceral. Legendary acting teacher Stella Adler described her protégé as 'the most keenly aware, the most empathetical human being alive'.

The best of times, the worst of times

It can be the best job in the world when you are doing what you love, enjoying the camaraderie and the thrill of putting together a great show with a talented bunch of actors, working as a team, challenging yourself physically, emotionally and spiritually. This goes some of the way to sustaining you through the down times, the months of unemployment, and barely making ends meet.

Live to act, or act to live?

This book should complement and consolidate your acting training, and maybe confirm and crystallise what you already hold true. Ideally it will provide a wake-up call that challenges you to take your acting career and your life in both hands and shake things up a bit, while

BLANCHETT IN ACTION

A FOCUSED CATE BLANCHETT WITH DIRECTOR RON HOWARD, ON SET FOR THE MOVIE *THE MISSING*, 2003.

still keeping a sense of perspective and fun, and acknowledging that acting, with all its idiosyncrasies, is merely a reflection of the crazy world in which we all live. It's no surprise that Cate Blanchett is at the top of her game, judging by her admirable talent and attitude: 'I live my life parallel with my work, and they are both equally important. I'm always amazed how much people talk about celebrity and fame. I don't understand the attraction.'

The rehearsal process can be exposing — but also helps make acting the most satisfying and exciting of career choices.

NO ANSWERS

What's it like being an actor? You'll never properly find out unless you give it a try. Nothing can prepare you for the extremes of joy and disappointment that acting can bring. If you think that 'people like me' don't become actors, you're almost certainly wrong. Just don't expect to find any answers! Your life and your career are there for the taking. Read this book in the spirit it was intended — as grist for the mill. Don't take it as gospel or base a philosophy around it. Take what you can, and move on. Live for the now and always be honest with yourself about what you really seek.

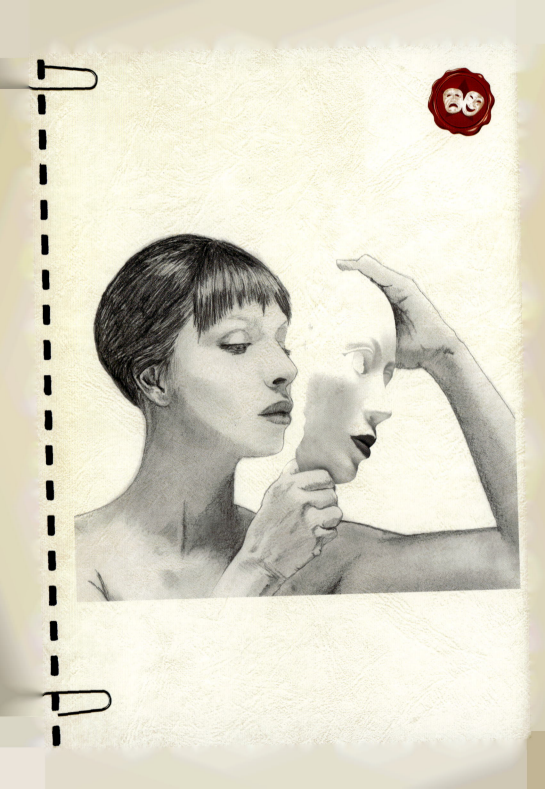

1

SO YOU WANT TO BE AN ACTOR?

Wanting to be an actor is an understandable dream. Those at the top seem to have it all – millions in the bank, a glamorous lifestyle and hordes of screaming fans – but deciding to pursue a career in acting is a major decision that will affect the rest of your life, not to mention those of your nearest and dearest. It's never too late or too early to start, but the advice actors often give to those entering this overcrowded profession is, 'If you want to do it, walk away, but if you have to do it, give it your all.'

> # Without wonder and insight, acting is just a trade. With it, it becomes creation.
>
> Bette Davis

WHY DO YOU WANT TO ACT?

The desire to perform is a curious affliction motivated by complicated urges. Jean-Paul Sartre described it as 'happy agony'. If you want to be an actor, no doubt acting means the world to you; you're passionate about it and you feel most alive when you're performing. You don't want to do anything else with your life and you want the freedom and flexibility of acting rather than the routine of nine to five. Welcome to the profession – in that respect, you are no different to every other actor.

SHAHRUKH KHAN

Khan has become one of the most successful actors in India. His secret? According to some in the know, his self-confidence, discipline, hard work and good public relations have outshone his evident talent.

FIND YOUR OWN GIGS

Be prepared to spend ninety per cent of your time either not working or doing acting jobs you don't really connect with. Even if you are a successful actor — getting the parts that really fire you up, with a great script, fantastic director, happy supportive cast, where everything clicks into place to create a commercial hit — those gigs rarely come round. Often you have to create your own projects to find fulfilment, even at the top.

Flipping acting

Many actors in their forties and beyond (even successful ones) long to quit the profession, but don't know what else to do. It's a crazy way to earn a living but crazy can be fun if you thrive on unpredictability and enjoy new challenges and pushing yourself, and so long as you avoid comparing yourself to everyone else (especially 'boring' non-actor friends climbing career ladders in other fields, three rungs at a time). Ninety-eight per cent of actors fail to earn a living wage from acting: you can earn more than the average actor by flipping burgers, and if you choose acting you may spend several months of every year doing exactly that! But don't let anyone stop you from following your dream. It's better to strike out than to spend your whole life wondering 'what if'.

Get what you deserve?

Acting is a meritocracy to the extent that, if you are *really* gifted and work at the right things, you will have more commercial success than your contemporaries. That's a very controversial thing to say, and it will probably offend many hard-working actors who are still slogging away in obscurity after 30 years. However, showbusiness *does* reward excellence… *eventually* – it's just that those rewards are few and far between and rarely proportionate to the effort invested and the sacrifices made along the way.

IT COULD BE YOU ONE DAY

A tourist tries her hands for size in Tom Hanks' handprints outside the famous Grauman's Chinese Theater in Hollywood, California.

> All my life, I always wanted to be somebody. Now I see that I should have been more specific.

Lily Tomlin

Knuckle down now

Still want to be an actor? Of course you do, because you love it and you're prepared to suffer the bad stuff. You're one of the top 0.01 per cent who will make it big and be happy. Hmmm… Well, you'd better roll your sleeves up right now, because it will take a gargantuan effort to get even halfway towards your goal.

Deliberate practice

The key to excellence in any field is 'deliberate practice', a concept that Geoff Colvin explores at length in *Talent is Overrated: What Really Separates World-Class Performers from Everybody Else*, a superb study of great achievers from Mozart to Tiger Woods: 'Across realms, the required concentration is so intense that it's exhausting. If deliberate practice is so hard – if in most cases it's "not inherently enjoyable", as some of the top researchers say – then why do some people put themselves through it day after day for decades, while most do not?'

THE OSCARS

Many actors dream of winning an Academy Award but the best reward is to love what you do rather than to chase accolades.

IS IT REALLY WORTH IT?

Colvin's book should be required reading for all actors (and anyone wishing to excel at anything). Read it, be brutally honest with yourself about your reasons for becoming a professional actor and then decide whether you are prepared to put in the necessary work to get what you want.

FAME? SHAME!

If you already have low self-esteem and want to 'be somebody' so that the world will sit up and take notice, get some therapy — it's cheaper and will make you happier than acting. Chasing fame is bad for your health! If you're in it for the fame, you'll be disappointed; no amount of fame will be enough, and when you have it you won't be able to control it or switch it off. A small amount of fame is nice enough. It's fun to get noticed and be appreciated, but when you experience adulation on the scale of Robert Pattinson, the world beyond your lonely hotel room becomes a crazy place and you have to be incredibly strong not to feel unworthy or go quietly mad.

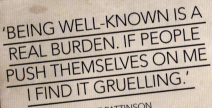

'BEING WELL-KNOWN IS A REAL BURDEN. IF PEOPLE PUSH THEMSELVES ON ME I FIND IT GRUELLING.'

ROBERT PATTINSON

With fame comes its cost — paparazzi, stalkers and lack of privacy. It becomes difficult to keep your feet on the ground.

A BUSINESS AND A CRAFT

You must understand that acting is a business and that you will be more successful if you treat it as such. The people who hire you may be creative types, but they are also businesspeople who need to make money, and if they think you can be relied upon to help them make money, they will hire you. As soon as you make this mind-shift, you will start marketing yourself more productively. You will also be more emotionally resilient and less likely to stray into the dangerous territory of defining your self-image and the core of your being as 'I, actor'.

TEN WAYS TO THINK LIKE A BUSINESSPERSON

1   Chances are you will not be 'discovered'. You have to make it happen by being proactive, focused and businesslike (as well as developing your acting technique and paying the bills). Don't expect your talent to do all the talking.

2   Presenting a businesslike image will impress employers more than your sensitivity, creativity and acting genius. Producer Thelma Holt looks for actors who exude a quiet confidence, and talent agent Marilyn Scott Murphy says, 'I prefer people to be at peace with themselves, comfortable and personable. A good disposition helps in this business.'

3   You are a product, so you need to be acutely aware of how you can be cast and typecast; otherwise, agents and casting directors won't know how to use you (see pages 200–201). Unless you can be pigeonholed, you won't get much work. This is reductive, lacks imagination and ignores versatility — but unfortunately it's the reality.

4   Ask others to sum you up in a single phrase and look around the industry to find other actors who are very similar to you, and who are already working, to help you find your niche and understand your type. Your actual type may not necessarily correspond to the type that you most enjoy playing.

(... continued overleaf)

Defining your self-image and seeing yourself as a product is one of the first steps to marketing yourself as an actor.

Keep your head screwed on

Some lucky actors are so gifted and commercial, and quickly create such a buzz in the industry, that their careers take off early despite any lack of business acumen or even social skills. To maintain their careers long-term, they need to make wise choices, but initially, at least, they don't have to worry about head shots, CVs, packaging and marketing themselves, showcasing, networking, landing an agent, contacting casting directors or going to open castings, because they suddenly find themselves at the centre of a feeding frenzy of top industry players. For the majority of actors, however, sound business, interpersonal and organisational skills are required from the get-go. Don't make the mistake of thinking that you can get by on talent and hard work alone.

Unless you are very lucky, every actor needs to begin with the basic marketing material — a carefully planned head shot is vital to casting success.

TEN WAYS TO THINK LIKE A BUSINESSPERSON (continued from page 16)

5   Seek out mentors who can guide your career and give you objective feedback on your strengths and weaknesses as an actor, and your type. Play to your strengths (ie, don't sell what you can't deliver) and work on your weaknesses.

6   Focus your efforts on the right acting industry professionals. Building a strong relationship with a few important players will get you further than sending out 200 CVs to 'Dear Sir/Madam'. If in 40 years' time you are taking stock of a successful career, you will probably attribute your success to a few key moments, and being championed by a handful of influential people. Plant your seeds where you want them to grow. Always be very focused and specific about how and where you target your energy, rather than market yourself to the whole world.

7   Stay on top of industry trends. Learn about your industry and the people in it, so you aren't betrayed by your ignorance. The author of this book once blew an important audition for the Royal Shakespeare Company by doing an audition speech for a prestigious director whose antipathy for the acting style he chose was well publicised. He was also unaware that the director had premièred the play 15 years earlier.

8   Set clear short-, medium- and long-term goals for your career. Ensure your goals are SMART:

S Specific **M** Measurable **A** Achievable
R Realistic **T** Timely

Then devise a five-year plan and a yearly plan to pursue your goals. Keep reviewing and revising the plan. Monitor your progress and be prepared to change your behaviour if things aren't working out. If doing the same thing leads to the same results and you don't like the results, you have to change what you're doing.

Keep organised — develop a weekly, monthly, even a yearly plan when you are starting out of showcases or performance possibilities.

TEN WAYS TO THINK LIKE A BUSINESSPERSON

9   Establish a reputation for being professional, reliable and consistent. People will hire you for these qualities over and above tortured/scruffy/beguiling/ impulsive/creative/genius.

10 Rejection is part of the game. Don't take it personally.

Behave professionally at all times during the audition process. A reputation for reliability and consistency is vital to the longevity of your career.

OVERNIGHT SUCCESS

In acting an overnight success is a rarity. For every Keira Knightley and Orlando Bloom, there are 50 Dustin Hoffmans, Al Pacinos, George Clooneys and Susan Sarandons who spent years performing under the radar before they hit the big time. And for every one of those, there are thousands more who slog away for years and never even earn a comfortable living.

INTERVENTIONS AND COINCIDENCES

It's important to sort yourself out at the start of your career, because the difference between success and failure can come down to a few bad choices at the beginning. Richard Thaler and Cass Sunstein bear this out in *Nudge*, their best-selling book about making choices: 'In many domains people are tempted to think, after the fact, that an outcome was entirely predictable, and that the success of a musician, an actor, an author, or a politician was inevitable in light of his or her skills and characteristics. Beware of that temptation. Small interventions and even coincidences, at a key stage, can produce large variations in the outcome.'

LATE BLOOMER

SUSAN SARANDON IN *JOE*, DIRECTED BY JOHN G. AVILDSEN, 1970
Joe was Sarandon's first major role. Despite working consistently for 18 years, it wasn't until her breakthrough with *Bull Durham* in 1988 that she became a household name.

Making good choices

Just because you haven't heard of an actor, doesn't mean they don't have an enviable career. However, if you don't cause a stir – at least within the profession – during the first few years of your career, you may remain at the same level for a long time or never break through. There are many talented actors competing for work, but your acting choices can make the difference between success and failure. Lots of talented actors struggle for recognition, but the ones who make the right choices early on, and have some luck, find employment. This allows them to learn even more, creating a virtuous loop, until after 20 years of consistent work with talented actors and directors, they leave their contemporaries far behind in terms of technique and material success.

Early bird gets the worm

Assimilate as much acting technique as possible and work hard in your early career. If you can be just 10 per cent better than your contemporaries at the beginning, there's a good chance that you'll be top of the pile 20 years down the line.

TREADING THE BOARDS

MICHAEL SHEEN IN *THE QUEEN*, DIRECTED BY STEPHEN FREARS, 2006

Sheen worked for 15 years successfully on the stage before landing large roles on screen.

WHO RISES TO THE SURFACE?

Michael Sheen came to the attention of mainstream US audiences with *The Queen*, *Frost/Nixon* and *Twilight: New Moon*, but he had already spent 15 years playing top theatre roles in Britain and on Broadway, as well as many TV and film roles. Jude Law enjoyed a decade of solid work before breaking through in *The Talented Mr Ripley*. In 1991, Anthony Hopkins cracked Hollywood when he won the Best Actor Oscar for *Silence of the Lambs*. Laurence Olivier had recognised his prodigious talent decades earlier, and subsequently Hopkins had spent years playing leading roles in top-flight stage productions and movies.

OVERNIGHT SUCCESS

TEN MYTHS ABOUT SHOWBUSINESS

1. People like me don't become actors

Actors come from all walks of life and backgrounds. You don't have to be young and beautiful or have parents in the business. It doesn't matter that you grew up in a small town in the middle of nowhere and don't know anybody in the business. The industry needs new talent all the time, and there's no reason why you shouldn't have the same crack of the whip as anyone else. There are no set rules, so if you are mentally tough, resourceful, prepared to work hard, keep learning, be flexible, personable and persistent, you will greatly increase your chance of success.

A STAR IN THE SHADOWS

RUFUS SEWELL AND KIM BASINGER IN *BLESS THE CHILD*, DIRECTED BY CHUCK RUSSELL, 2000
Although he remains in relative obscurity, Rufus Sewell has starred in many well-known movies – including *A Knight's Tale*, *Helen of Troy*, *Tristan & Isolde* and *The Holiday*.

2. Being a fantastic actor is all I need to succeed

There are very few significant talents languishing in obscurity within the industry (eg, Iain Glen, Rufus Sewell and Fiona Shaw are less well known to the general public than many soap opera stars, but they are widely acknowledged as three of the most gifted actors in Britain). If you are 1-in-1,000 extraordinary you will be spotted quickly, but even the most talented actors rarely appear on the scene as a fully formed hot property. Some get a head start for commercial reasons, and this gives them the opportunity to develop and grow, but the majority put in many years to hone their craft. Then, when they break through to become a household name, everyone mistakenly thinks they are an overnight success.

3. You have to climb over others to get to the top

There are a few nasty people working in any industry who think nothing of cheating or bullying others, but being nice, friendly, trustworthy, honest and outward-looking will get you much further than being selfish, stamping on people and being self-obsessed. Be nice to everyone, if for no other reason than that today's runner, making the tea, could be tomorrow's movie producer. Acting is a cooperative process that thrives on teamwork.

You do not have be cruel to create your own opportunities in the business.

4. All actors are extroverts

Many actors are shy and introverted (which some would argue makes them better observers), but enjoy expressing themselves through acting. Being shy can be a hindrance in an industry where effective communication is at a premium, but it shouldn't prevent you from becoming an actor. You can still be shy and achieve your goals, so long as you work on your attitude towards social situations.

5. Acting training will destroy your naturalness

Good acting training opens up a whole new world of possibilities. If you are resistant to developing your existing skills and learning new ones, you probably won't get very far as an actor anyway.

Actor training will not destroy your natural ability — acting requires technique as well as talent.

6. Actors make big money

A handful of A-listers make millions, but the vast majority of actors barely scrape a living, including many of those who appear regularly on TV in minor roles. Most of the A-listers who now command huge fees spent at least 10 years earning very modest sums, with no guarantee of eventual success. Try not to measure your success in terms of fame and money, because there's a strong chance that if you choose to be an actor you will spend many years broke.

7. Acting is easy

Experienced actors make acting look easy, but it takes years of practice to acquire the skills that allow them to look effortless. It's hard work that takes stamina and resilience. Filming, while lucrative, is especially demanding. Al Pacino describes filming as 'an exhausting experience – not just the acting itself [but] the being uprooted from where you are and sitting seven or eight hours in a camper. As Orson Welles said, that's really what you are paid for.'

You may need to take on part-time work to supplement your income as an actor.

8. Acting is glamorous

It is and it isn't. Being a high-profile guest at a red-carpet première can be exciting and glamorous, but, wherever you are in your career, you are always part of a pecking order, looking at those above you and maybe envying what you think they have, and looking down on those beneath you, fearing that this job is your last. The atmosphere at the Oscars is awash with vanity and insecurity – everyone clinging to their little bit of status, trying to show up at the right parties and be seen with the right people. Or it can be fun and exciting if you adopt the right attitude! Success can be glamorous, but, like being a top sportsperson, the actual day-to-day job of acting is not – it's hard work, sometimes boring, involving many hours of training and years without recognition or reward.

Work hard to become the best actor you can be, and let the glamour and awards take care of themselves.

9. People are impressed when I tell them I'm an actor

Don't be so sure. We live in a world that increasingly venerates celebrity, but most people couldn't care less whether you are an actor. So don't assume that everyone will be impressed by what you do, or even that your friends (or those guys at school who said you'd never amount to anything) will remember or bother to watch you when you get on TV. Act because you love it, and don't put yourself on a pedestal. Keep it real, take a genuine interest in people and stop looking to others for self-validation.

10. As long as I am persistent, I will succeed

True, so long as you persist at the right things. Persistence means learning from your mistakes, finding out what works, discarding what doesn't, having the courage to admit to yourself when you need a change of direction and seeking honest and objective feedback from knowledgeable people whom you trust. Persistence without flexibility is narrow-minded cowardice.

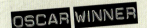

GRACE KELLY WINS AN ACADEMY AWARD FOR *THE COUNTRY GIRL*, 1954

Grace Kelly seems the ultimate example of glamorous stardom. The race for the Oscar in 1954 became a heightened media frenzy. The glamorous Kelly won the award while Judy Garland, who was aiming for a comeback award for her performance in *A Star Is Born*, was in the hospital giving birth to her son.

2
THE ACTOR

This chapter introduces you to the basic principles that underpin modern acting. It addresses some common mistakes and misconceptions, as well as highlighting the qualities that distinguish great actors from their peers. Acting demands acute observation, empathy, self-knowledge, childlike curiosity, attention to detail, relaxed concentration, the ability constantly to challenge your assumptions and make brave choices and a commitment to serve the script. This is all supported by a sophisticated technique that takes years of training and practice to make your own.

> The actor's art cannot be taught. He must be born with ability; but the technique, through which his talent can find expression – that can and must be taught.
>
> Richard Boleslavsky

THE IMPORTANCE OF TECHNIQUE

Technique is not acting; it is a framework that supports an actor's talent. Just as a ballet dancer must work at the barre and the pianist must practise scales, actors gain command of their medium by acquiring technique. However, technique should not make you more technical, but more free, and gives you the foundation to make brave choices.

Technique isn't about finding the 'right' way to act; it's more useful to think of it as eliminating all the hundreds of wrong ways, the acquired habits and obstacles that hamper even the most talented actors. It isn't enough to trust nature and act by instinct, just as you wouldn't expect to become the fastest sprinter in the world through natural ability and a winning attitude.

Exploring different techniques and methods can help the actor to achieve a deeper connection and correct bad habits.

CREATE YOUR OWN PATH

There are many different ways to learn acting. Even the techniques described in this book can only scratch the surface of the possibilities. Some acting techniques will work for you; others will leave you cold. Everybody learns through a different combination of factors (intellectual, emotional, physical) and through exploration and repetition, and everybody's path is different, so trust your instincts, leave yourself open to change and try to make everything you learn your own.

PROFESSIONAL APPROACH

During the early part of his career, the Jamaican sprinter Usain Bolt relied on his natural ability to beat his competitors, and didn't take athletics too seriously. But he only became the best in the world (by a significant margin) after he developed a professional approach and worked diligently on his technique. This raised the stakes for him — there's always more to lose when you put more of yourself into something — but it also raised the rewards.

Explore your choices

Technique helps you to focus on specifics rather than get stuck with generalisations, to explore lots of choices rather than take instant decisions, and to recognise the complexities and contradictions of being human. It gives you the tools and confidence to reach out to meet the characters you will play at the very limits of their extraordinary lives rather than shrink them to fit you. You may be lucky enough to have an adequate acting career for a few years on talent alone, but if you want to be the best you need to develop your technique throughout your life.

Become an avid reader of both classical and contemporary plays and visit the theatre or the cinema at least once a week.

"It's a business you go into because you're an egocentric It's a very embarrassing profession."

Katharine Hepburn

THE DESIRE TO PLEASE

In *An Actor Prepares*, Stanislavski describes an exercise in which acting students are required to go up onto the bare stage. The director explains: 'The curtain goes up, and you are sitting on the stage. You are alone. You sit and sit and sit... At last the curtain comes down again. That is the whole play. Nothing simpler could be imagined, could it?'

Each student takes a turn, but without a purpose they all feel awkward, embarrassed. One student explains how 'part of me sought to entertain the onlookers, so that they would not become bored; another part told me to pay no attention to them.' When he watched the others, 'their helplessness and desire to please were ridiculous'.

LUNACHARSKY, STANISLAVKSI & SHAW

This image, taken in 1931 in Moscow, shows the powerful figure in theatre Stanislavski had become, flanked by the playwright George Bernard Shaw and the Russian culture and education minister Anatoly Lunacharsky.

The desire to please, and to 'perform', has diminished many a promising young actor. Those awkward students were being watched by an audience, so they felt the necessity to do something, to be entertaining, and ultimately to please the director, but since they had nothing to do, they were lost.

Suddenly the director announces he will repeat the experiment. He invites the first student, Maria, onto the stage again, but then he pretends to look for something in his notebook. Maria sits 'motionless, with her eyes fixed on him. She was afraid she might disturb him, and she merely waited for further orders. Her pose was life-like, natural.' The curtain falls, and the director explains that Maria was at ease on stage because she didn't 'act' anything, but she was still doing something – she was waiting while trying not to disturb him. Her body was motionless and yet her whole being was in action. She was unaware of the audience but she was real and truthful because she was pursuing a want, playing an action.

FOCUS ON WANTS

Every moment you are on stage or in front of a camera, you must be focused on what you (ie, the character you are playing) want, and pursue those wants through action (which is not the same thing as movement, as Maria's second attempt demonstrates). Any time you feel awkward, it is a sure sign that you aren't doing this, and if you are in front of an audience (or an acting teacher) your desire to please will quickly lead you into tricks and clichés and you will cease to be truthful.

The actor at ease — motionless, waiting. Stanislavski's exercise proves how playing an action is key to authentic performance.

> ## Don't you see!? We're actors – we're the opposite of people!
>
> Tom Stoppard, *Rosencrantz and Guildenstern Are Dead*

RELAXATION AND CONCENTRATION

Unnecessary tension in the body always limits an actor's performance.

All great actors have mastered the secret of relaxed concentration. It is probably the single most important skill an actor can possess, but it is also one of the most misunderstood concepts. The feeling of ease for the actor isn't merely the elimination of tension; otherwise, jellyfish would be acting legends. It requires self-analysis to recognise how your body responds to tension, where, when and how you generate it. Everyone's tension patterns are unique. Tension doesn't just happen – you create it, and it begins in your mind.

What is relaxation?

It can take many months of movement and acting classes to learn to recognise where you hold tension, to free up problem areas, and to address your habitual tension patterns. Some are defence mechanisms (eg, some people, especially men, puff out their chests

RELAX YOUR EYES

Many actors may feel relaxed in mind and body, but carry their tension in their eyes, often consciously, because they mistakenly believe that they are somehow generating intensity and presence with them. By focusing on externals these bulgy-eyed actors only succeed in alienating their audience, who recognise that real people don't walk around with their eyes on stalks. What tension do you generate through your preconceptions, and where?

FEAR AND LACK OF TRUST

Tension and our habitual responses are often caused by fear and lack of trust in ourselves. Our preconceptions, as a person and as an actor, can also create tension and appear untruthful. One of your main responsibilities as an actor is to be a believable human being (or whatever organism the script demands), so always beware of hiding behind tension. Of course, you can't 'act' believable — this is only achieved through pursuing what your character wants through action, while in a state of relaxed concentration.

Tall people often slouch in order to compensate for their height — this is bad practice which is easily remedied.

CHARACTER TENSION

Some actors build an excess of physical tension into their characterisations — this gives them the reward of feeling that they are working hard (often too hard, and at the wrong things), but it can also give them something to hide behind. Then they wonder why they are locked down and can't access their emotions, or live in the moment. Don't adopt tension as a character choice. Express character through your wants and actions, and beware of mistaking body tension for an expression of a personality trait. If you feel tense on stage, it is usually because you aren't actively pursuing your character's wants.

when they greet a stranger); others are created to compensate for self-image (tall people slouching to disguise their height, short people standing upright). All these actions cause tension and hamper imaginative expression. For sure, actors need a relaxed and open body so they can breathe properly to support the voice, but many relaxation exercises work on tension in a purely mechanical way without addressing the underlying motivations and misconceptions that cause it.

RELAXATION AND CONCENTRATION | 35

> When an actor is completely absorbed by some profoundly moving objective so that he throws his whole being passionately into its execution, he reaches a state we call inspiration.
>
> *Constantin Stanislavski*

THE METHOD

Many contradictory myths have sprung up in popular culture around actors who use 'The Method' – primarily, that they are difficult to work with, being either perfectionist prima donnas or moody slobs who forget and/or mumble their lines – but it is simply a repeatable technique that offers actors a set of tools to find realism and avoid the temptation of theatrical tricks and clichés in fashion at a given time. Its origins were in Moscow in the early twentieth century, but it continues to evolve today as it is taught at drama schools around the world.

THE MOSCOW STATE THEATRE, 1899

Russian playwright Anton Chekhov top, third from left, together with actors of the Moscow State Theatre, founded by Stanislavski in 1898.

Constantin Stanislavski and the Moscow Art Theatre

Born in Russia in 1863, when melodramatic, effect-seeking acting was in vogue, Stanislavski passionately believed in 'spiritual realism' or living the part, exploring the truth of character and situation, and responsive interaction with other actors, rather than adopting the shallow theatrical tricks and conventions of his contemporaries. In 1898, he co-founded the Moscow Art Theatre with theatre director Vladimir Nemirovich-Danchenko and a company of 39 actors where he developed his systematic approach to training actors, including a repertoire of technical exercises. He wrote several works that every actor should read: *An Actor Prepares, Building a Character, Creating a Role* and *My Life in Art.*

MEMORIES AND IMAGINATION

Stanislavski was the first person to recognise that acting requires dedication and discipline, and that actors need training. He encouraged actors to use their own memories and imagination to express emotions and later approached truthful emotion through physical action. His approach demanded rigorous self-analysis and critique designed to give the actors access to their own subconscious to unlock emotions. The ensemble ethos was key, supported by extensive research and detailed rehearsals in which every action was meticulously analysed. The result was a detailed psychological realism achieved through the quest for technical perfection.

CHEKHOV AND 'THE METHOD'

THE SEAGULL, ANTON PAVLOVICH CHEKHOV
Hattie Morahan and Ben Whishaw star in The National Theatre's performance of *The Seagull* in 2006. The play premièred at the Moscow Art Theatre in 1898, directed by Stanislavski.

Richard Boleslavsky and the American Laboratory Theater

Stanislavski's method reached America thanks to the Polish actor and film director Richard Boleslavsky, who studied at the Moscow Art Theatre. After the Russian Revolution, he directed some movies in his native Poland, then arrived in New York in the early 1920s, founded the American Laboratory Theater, and invited fellow émigré and Moscow Art Theatre actor Maria Ouspenskaya to teach with him. One of his students was Lee Strasberg.

'LOVE ART IN YOURSELF AND NOT YOURSELF IN ART.'
CONSTANTIN STANISLAVSKI

Lee Strasberg and the Group Theater

When the Moscow Art Theatre visited America in 1923, Strasberg was blown away by the actors' professionalism, cohesion, lack of ego and their ability to live the inner life of their characters. This encounter crystallised his life's vocation – to develop these techniques into a

BOLESLAVKY'S DIRECTION

GRETA GARBO AND HERBERT MARSHALL IN *THE PAINTED VEIL*, 1934, RICHARD BOLESLAVSKY.

coherent system for American actors. He attended Boleslavsky's classes and in 1931 he founded the Group Theater, with director Harold Clurman, where he developed the technique that has come to be known as The Method or Method Acting. The cornerstones of this collective approach were improvisation and emotional memory (see pages 94–95 and 42–43). Everything was secondary to the driving force of true emotion and working from the 'inside out'. According to Clurman, Strasberg's method achieved drama in which 'a constant conflict [is] so held in check that a kind of beautiful spareness results.'

'A TRUE TECHNIQUE'

Another essential branch of Method acting was developed by the three-time Tony Award-winning German-born American actor and teacher Uta Hagen, who credited Harold Clurman for unlocking her desire 'to find a true technique of acting, how to make a character flow through me'. She taught at the HB Studio in Greenwich Village in New York City for many years and published her techniques in *Respect for Acting* and *A Challenge for the Actor*. One of the most highly respected acting coaches in Britain, Doreen Cannon, trained under her in New York and then spent 30 years teaching in London at the Drama Centre and RADA. Since her untimely death in the early 1990s, her daughter Dee Cannon has become one of the most sought-after acting coaches in the world.

STAR METHOD ACTORS IN PERFORMANCE

LEE STRASBERG AND AL PACINO IN *AND JUSTICE FOR ALL*, 1979, NORMAN JEWISON Strasberg trained Al Pacino at the Actors Studio in New York. Here they star together in the Academy Award-nominated courtroom drama.

Stella Adler

Method acting didn't stop with Strasberg. The most famous method actor of them all, Marlon Brando, gave Strasberg little credit for his professional development. He was trained primarily by Stella Adler (who also coached Warren Beatty and Robert De Niro), an actress at the Group Theater who conflicted with Strasberg in her belief that the actor's imagination is more important than emotion. She devised exercises to develop the imagination and returned to the text, human growth and the constant study of human behaviour. She taught that acting was doing, and giving oneself over to the given circumstances of the text and the scene rather than digging into past memories. Her mantras were 'In your choice is your talent' and 'We are what we do, not what we say.' She reclaimed an actor's need, and right, to make strong independent acting choices rather than follow a rigid code laid down by others.

MEISNER TECHNIQUE

Ex-Group Theater actor, and teacher at the Actors Studio, Sanford Meisner focused on exercises that develop 'moment-to-moment' spontaneity, 'riding the river of impulses', acting as reacting rather than aiming for a predetermined result. The most fundamental exercise in the Meisner Technique is called Repetition, and he encouraged actors to learn lines by rote without inflection, to avoid fixating on a sound or thought. Well-known actors trained in the Meisner Technique include Kim Basinger, Jeff Goldblum, Sam Rockwell and Christopher Lloyd.

'THE ACTORS STUDIO MEANT SO MUCH TO ME IN MY LIFE... THAT WAS A REMARKABLE TURNING POINT IN MY LIFE. IT WAS DIRECTLY RESPONSIBLE FOR GETTING ME TO QUIT ALL THOSE JOBS AND JUST STAY ACTING.'

AL PACINO

The mural outside the Stella Adler Academy highlighting its star quality on Highland Avenue in West Hollywood, California.

THE ACTORS STUDIO

In 1947, Elia Kazan (who directed Brando in *A Streetcar Named Desire* and *On The Waterfront*, and James Dean in *East of Eden*) and several members of the Group Theater founded the Actors Studio, a non-profit workshop for professional actors, and Strasberg quickly became its artistic director. It fostered a new generation of acting stars, including Al Pacino, Dustin Hoffman, Paul Newman, Anne Bancroft, James Dean, Jack Nicholson, Jane Fonda, Sally Field and Marilyn Monroe.

DIRECTOR'S CUT

JAMES DEAN IN *EAST OF EDEN*, 1955, ELIA KAZAN
Director Elia Kazan collaborated with Lee Strasberg. The movie's star, James Dean, was quoted as saying that The Actors Studio was 'the best thing that can happen to an actor'.

The idea is you learn to use everything that happened in your life and you learn to use it in creating the character you're working on. You learn to dig into your unconscious and make use of every experience you ever had.

Marlon Brando

> There has to be some part of a human being that I feel I can slice open and say, 'Look at this.' And some people in the audience can say, 'I don't live in that space, but I've passed through it.' That emotional response is why we do the job. If you don't have that effect on people, the actually what are you doing?
>
> Adrian Lester

EMOTIONAL MEMORY

How does an actor cry, scream with genuine fear, laugh or get angry at will? Ideally the impetus comes naturally, because you are fully involved on stage, you are totally immersed in the reality of the play and everyone is in the zone. But there will be many times when the other actors give you nothing, or you have to make an entrance in a heightened emotional state. Maybe you've been sitting in your trailer on a film set for five hours and then have to access powerful emotions for a 30-second take. Some actors seem able to tune in emotionally at will, but most of us have been conditioned to suppress these emotions, so this technique can unlock them for you organically when required.

AFFECTIVE MUSIC

Music can elicit a powerful emotional response in most people, even when it has no associations with a past event in their life. Many actors listen to music off stage to prepare themselves for a scene, but you can use emotional memory triggers during performance, as well.

'IT'S IMPORTANT NOT TO INDICATE. PEOPLE DON'T TRY TO SHOW THEIR FEELINGS, THEY TRY TO HIDE THEM.'

ROBERT DE NIRO

LOOK TO YOUR PAST

Emotional memory is the recall of an event in your life that produced a strong emotional response. If you want to find an emotional memory for crying, laughter, fear or anger, choose a moment in your past when you felt one of these emotions. Only use events you have come to terms with and avoid any that are still raw, because you need to be able to control the emotions rather than become self-indulgent or, worse, compound any deep psychological trauma.

Returning to a memory will help to identify the trigger for an emotional response.

Emotional memory can be used to trigger any emotion from guilt or embarrassment to fear and anger.

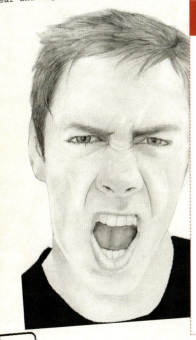

FIND THE TRIGGER

Lie down, close your eyes and run through the incident in your mind in minute detail. Try to recreate the surroundings, the sounds, smells and objects that were present (it may help to describe the event to a friend). After 30 minutes or more of acute forensic attention, you should reach a trigger point that will cause you to cry, laugh, get angry. If this catalyst isn't immediately apparent, repeat the exercise until you find it — it could be a snippet of music, a look someone gave you, an object, a taste or smell, but it will always be the same. Identify the trigger and you will be able to use it to generate this specific emotional response at will. You may be able to use the same one for the rest of your career, or it might wear out in a week. That's why it is important to develop a repertoire of different emotional triggers to draw upon. But remember: just because you feel an emotion doesn't mean you have to show it.

SENSE MEMORY

Sense memory is the recall of physical sensations – not emotional sensations, although they often cause an emotional response – such as heat, cold, nausea, fatigue, hunger or intoxication. Its success relies on exploring specific details.

Explore the specifics

Is it dry heat or humid? Where on your body do you feel hot? Maybe your earlobes are burning, your scalp feels prickly, the back of your throat is dry, or your underarms are wet and sticky. Now compensate for these physical sensations: rub your ears, ruffle your hair, swallow, ease your elbows outwards to unstick the fabric of your shirt from your armpits. These actions will actually strengthen the physical sensations (but remember that you are *not* doing this to show an audience you are hot).

If the scene requires you to feel tired, ask yourself what the specific circumstances are that have caused your fatigue. Working at a computer for three hours without a break causes a different kind of weariness to walking ten miles in thick snow. In the former, your eyes might be sore, shoulders tense, the backs of your legs tingling and numb, because you have been sitting down for so long. In the latter, the balls of your feet might be aching, your ankles soaking wet, lungs burning, you may have a sore patch between your legs where the tops of your thighs have chafed together. You may even feel invigorated despite your fatigue – see how interesting your inner life becomes when you explore specifics!

These actors, portraying a sensory reaction to the cold, have focused on keeping their clothes wrapped round them, and warming their feet.

When people are drunk, they often try to hide it. Don't 'act' drunkenness — focus instead on combatting its effects.

BEING DRUNK

Drunkenness often gives away the inexperienced actor. If you need to be drunk in a scene, focus on the specific circumstances. Which stage of drunkenness are you in, how does it affect specific parts of your body and what do you do to compensate? For example, when you are very inebriated, you may find it hard to stop your head from flopping, or perhaps your eyes go out of focus. Concentrate on keeping your head straight and your eyes focused, and you will start to feel drunk. Don't choose these examples, though — pick your own personal bodily responses (according to the prior circumstances) and then compensate for them. Don't telegraph this to the audience; most drunks try to appear sober.

> # He's a perfectionist, obsessed with detail. That's why he went over budget and over schedule.
>
> Leonardo Di Caprio on working with Martin Scorsese in *Gangs of New York*

OBSERVATION

Creativity and originality in any sphere thrive on three things: detail, detail, detail. Another famous Leonardo (da Vinci) spent hour upon hour dissecting cadavers because he was passionate about understanding how the human body worked. Driven by relentless curiosity, he tirelessly gathered input by observing the world, because he knew that the imagination can only soar when it is grounded in specifics. It takes time and constant practice to challenge your own assumptions and go beyond the non-reflective experiencing of daily life.

Get real!

Continue to observe and embrace your inner life, but cultivate a genuine interest in people. If you want to be an actor so you can rise above the sweating masses and grab yourself a mansion in the Hollywood Hills, good luck with that. An easier route would be to get therapy for your narcissistic personality disorder, climb down from your pedestal and muck in with everybody else. You'll have a happier life, too.

> 'I'M CURIOUS ABOUT OTHER PEOPLE. THAT'S THE ESSENCE OF MY ACTING. I'M INTERESTED IN WHAT IT WOULD BE LIKE TO BE YOU.'
>
> MERYL STREEP

USE NATURAL CURIOSITY

Observation isn't just about watching how someone walks or thinking about their speech patterns. Try to understand why they behave like they do and, if you can't figure it out, make logical and intuitive decisions based on your observations. Often, you'll make discoveries that are polar opposites of what you would expect. The more you look for the subtext of life (and dialogue in a script), the less you will settle for easy answers in your work. Above all, allow yourself to be driven by curiosity. Be a magpie, collecting ideas and information and always observing — but, unlike the magpie, have regular mental and spiritual clearouts, since sometimes you have to throw away a ladder once you have climbed it.

OBSERVING FOR YOUR ROLE

Many actors think they can imagine themselves into a part, but this imagination must be based on concrete observation. At the end of *The Matrix*, Neo stops seeing the construct of the world around him and sees only the code, the building blocks that lie underneath. Make it your mission always to dig beneath the surface. The world becomes a truly fascinating place when you become an expert reader of subtext. You'll start to see people, objects and ideas in relation to each other, rather than in isolation or simply how they relate to you.

Careful observation is the key to truthful expression in acting. Watch how people move, talk, interact and especially what they want or try to conceal.

> Your scene, or part, is a long string of beads – beads of action. You play with them as you play with a rosary. You can start anywhere, any time, and go as far as you wish, if you have a good hold on the beads themselves.
>
> *Richard Boleslavsky*

DRAMATIC ACTION

Acting is what characters do, not what they feel. Your actions map out the character's journey through the play, and ultimately they serve the story, which has been written by the playwright or scriptwriters. The dramatic action of a story must always move forward and, as an actor, your character's dramatic action is always about overcoming obstacles in order to pursue what your character wants. Drama is the result of characters being unable to achieve their objectives.

When reading a script you can identify dramatic action in terms of conflicting objectives.

SERVING THE TEXT

Theatre and film are rarely a naturalistic *tranche de vie*, because the dramatist has selected the events in the story, the significance of which are revealed by the actors. In the seminal *Norman Conquests*, Alan Ayckbourn treats the audience to three plays, where we see the same characters and events from a different vantage point: dining room, living room and garden of the same house. This demonstrates that events are not important in themselves, but in their significance and impact on the characters and the audience (which is why in Greek drama so many of the dramatic events are allowed to take place off stage). Keep this in mind and you will always come back to the dramatic arc, the plot, the text — that's what directors and actors mean when they talk about 'serving the text'.

THREE PLAYS IN ONE

THE NORMAN CONQUESTS, ALAN AYCKBOURN
Amelia Bullmore and Ben Miles star in the 2008 Old Vic, London, production of *The Norman Conquests*.

Play the action

The challenge for the actor is to make those wants big enough that they tell a compelling story. Nothing must detract from the action, which is why you must always play the want and not your emotional state. The emotion arises spontaneously from pursuing your character's objectives and making sure that the objectives and the obstacles are strong. The stronger they are, the more dramatic the action.

Serve the plot

We have said that you must serve the story, but actually you are serving the plot. The plot is the text of the play, which contains only the significant events in the overall story that the dramatist has chosen to include in the play. It will include the most important moments of crisis, the points in the story where the characters have to make life-changing decisions under maximum pressure.

COMMON MISTAKES MADE BY INEXPERIENCED ACTORS

Many actors believe that their talent and spontaneity will take them wherever they want to go, so they neglect other areas of their career, such as constantly developing their technique, improving their organisational, business and people skills and being proactive. Inexperienced actors concentrate on how they feel, while experienced actors focus on what they want to make the other characters in the scene feel. Trust in the truth of your identification with the character rather than trying to be interesting. Being interesting is representational, follows fashion and is empty; truthful is arresting and timeless.

'IF YOU GIVE AN AUDIENCE A CHANCE THEY WILL DO HALF YOUR ACTING FOR YOU.'

KATHARINE HEPBURN

Negative capability

Always simplify, but don't grasp for easy answers. Despite the inevitable time restraints of rehearsal, the longer you can resist the urge to 'deliver the goods', the greater your chance of discovering something really special. John Keats famously called this state 'negative capability', the ability to be 'in uncertainties, mysteries, doubts without any irritable reaching after fact and reason'.

During the rehearsal process, you will be given a huge number of notes about your performance. Learn to take all notes and not be defensive.

TAKE CRITICISM

Welcome criticism (rather than reassurance). Ask people to be honest rather than massage your ego. Even acting teachers — except the very good ones — will be diplomatic, rather than tell you what you need to hear. Demonstrate to people that you can handle and welcome critical feedback. You need to know the bad habits that detract from your truth. Many actors are over-anxious to communicate or to present an image to an audience. They may even believe they are being generous and giving of themselves, but the result is they push the audience away. Don't send out to an audience. Invite them in.

Learning to take constructive direction is an important part of the acting process.

My teacher gave me the best advice and I've never forgotten it. He told me, 'Hang on to your bollocks and just do it.' I took him to mean that it was one thing having a bit of talent but you need to work at it and not be scared to take on challenges if you're going to get anywhere.

Ben Whishaw

COMMON MISTAKES MADE BY INEXPERIENCED ACTORS

3
THE ACTOR'S QUESTIONS

When preparing for a role, an actor asks six questions. The detailed search for the answers during rehearsals and many hours of individual preparation enables you to achieve complete integration with the inner life of the character and the strong forces that drive you. You're permanently pursuing a powerful want, not an emotion, and there's always someone or something stopping you – you think thoughts that compel you into action and conflict with yourself and others. Conflicting needs and obstacles create the drama.

WHO AM I?

After you have read the script a few times and have understood its purpose, main themes and plot, the first question an actor must ask is 'Who am I?' The whole of the next chapter is dedicated to answering this question, but the key principle to keep in mind while you explore character is this: whatever you do must always correspond truthfully to the needs and intentions of the script. Many actors make the mistake of exploring their character (or perform audition speeches) without understanding their character's function in the story.

Pursuing your character's wants moment-to-moment leads to truthful dramatic action.

Get with the plot

Read the script again and work out how each character contributes to telling the story. Identify the main protagonists who drive the story and those who are involved in subplots. Assimilate the plot as simply as you can, and see how your character fits into the story, and your character arc: how, when and why does the character change and develop during the story? Hold on to this information. Don't skip ahead to explore your inner life until you understand your storytelling function.

ALWAYS SERVE THE TEXT

The character lives in a world created by the playwright and projected through dialogue and relationships. Every bit of detailed character work must serve the telling of the story. If you keep this at the front of your mind, you will avoid self-serving tangents that detract from this goal. There is no merit or reward in creating a real and deeply lived character who doesn't serve the text.

Me, me, me

From the moment you are cast, stop referring to the character as 'he' or 'she'. Asking 'Who am I?' is very different from 'Who is (s)he?' The 'I' is fundamental because you will need to draw on your own life experience, thoughts and emotions to identify imaginatively with the inner life of your character. This is not an intellectual exercise. In the end you only have yourself to work with, although you do have everybody in you, so from now on the character is 'I' and you must feed your imagination throughout the creative process by using the magic 'If I…'

FIND YOUR CHARACTER'S INNER LIFE

It is your job to illuminate the character, to give them an inner emotional life, and a physical life. The audience can only be emotionally engaged by the story when they observe human beings in all their subtleties and complexities.

'THAT'S WHY WE'RE HERE – TO SERVE THIS ENTIRE STORY.'

MERYL STREEP

WHERE AM I?

All living creatures interact with their environment and they are physically and emotionally affected by it. It isn't enough to know that the scene takes place in a drawing room, Dunsinane Castle, or the planet Mars. You must research the environment of every scene in specific detail – the sounds, smells and textures. Your reality as an actor is reinforced by detailed knowledge of your surroundings, which also influence the way you communicate and function within them, especially since 'Where am I' isn't about a physical place – it includes society and culture.

When being filmed in front of a green screen actors must be able to use their imagination to establish a strong sense of place.

Create a sensory storeroom

You cannot rely on the set alone to fill in the details of your surroundings, because no set design will supply you with as much detail as your own research. Even when you are shooting on location, you may be using green screen, so you need to imagine your reality even more. Besides, to do this is missing the point completely as to how you create your surroundings; they are not something you bolt on at the end, like the lighting or other technical effects. You cannot create a living character in a vacuum, so your surroundings, including props, clothes and other concrete aspects of your environment, are a sensory repository which you must incorporate into your work from the beginning.

ENVIRONMENT INFLUENCES ACTION

Imagine you are playing a scene in a bus stop in a run-down neighbourhood. There's graffiti on the walls, broken glass on the floor, a smell of urine. It's just rained, so the concrete pavement is wet and shiny. There's a puddle at your feet, the red plastic seat is wet and the wind occasionally gusts past. All this input feeds your inner life and reinforces your reality, and also gives you the opportunity to explore character. For example, before sitting down you might take out your handkerchief and wipe the seat clean and dry; you might use your sleeve to wipe the seat, sit blithely in the wet or remain standing (which makes you feel irritated). In this example, imagining a wet seat offers lots of character choices, made possible by being specific about your surroundings. The more detail you use to answer the question 'Where am I?' the more choices will be available to you during the scene. You also need to know the previous circumstances — where you just came from and what happened there.

Your environment influences you physically and this in turn can affect the way you feel. It also allows you to explore different character choices.

WHEN AM I?

When doesn't just refer to the time of day or night – it also locates you somewhere on a timeline, past, present or future. Your character lives in a social and moral landscape that is both geographical ('where am I?') and temporal ('when am I?').

Get in the time zone

Immerse yourself in the period in which your character lives – the sounds, the smells, the textures, tastes, clothes, language and social norms. Look at old photographs, watch documentaries and read chronicles or diaries. You can even use relatively recent and well-respected movies, but be aware that movies are of their time, so if, for example, you watch Charlton Heston's *Ben Hur*, you'll see a version of Roman life filtered through the lens of the late 1950s. But it can still give you a flavour, a mood, and anything that feeds your imagination is good, especially listening to music from the period.

Leafing through old photographs can help contextualise your performance.

Avoid clichés

The time period will affect how you express yourself and relate to other people. Unless you develop a rich and accurately researched understanding of the period, you won't be able to identify fully with the character, and you may end up resorting to generalisations, such as a stiff and formal physicality, exaggerated articulation or artificial lyricism in your speech. These clichés may fool you into thinking that you

BEFORE THE PLAY BEGINS

Act I of *The Cherry Orchard* opens in the early morning hours of a day in May, just after the turn of the twentieth century, Act II opens in midsummer, and several months have passed by the beginning of Act III. The final act takes place several weeks later. As an actor in this play, you would need to know what has brought you to each moment (from birth), as well as what happens between the scenes and acts. But you would also need to look even further back in time, and research, for example, the emancipation of the serfs in 1861, because one of the main themes of the play is the effects of this social change on the characters.

HISTORICAL CONTEXT

ETHAN HAWKE IN ANTON CHEKHOV'S *THE CHERRY ORCHARD*, DIRECTED BY SAM MENDES, THE OLD VIC, LONDON, 2009.

are 'getting' the period, but they won't enrich your inner life, and these shallow impositions will actually hamper your creativity.

Time is your lifeline

Time, for the actor, is not simply an intellectual exercise or a textual detail – it is literally your lifeline. If the action takes place at eight o'clock on a late summer evening, the previous events of the day, week, month or season impact on the wants and choices of your present.

WHAT DO I WANT?

Human beings are driven by needs. They pursue these needs through words and actions. The stronger your needs, and the greater the obstacles that stop you getting them, the greater the drama.

Superobjective

Your superobjective is the single want that governs your entire life (although your character might not know it consciously). It could be 'to die' or 'to find true love' or 'to take over the world'. Some actors prefer to consider several overall character objectives rather than a single superobjective.

SCENE OBJECTIVES

Keeping your superobjective in mind, study the script and identify your major need or objective for each scene in the play or movie. This major objective should be linked to events and move the dramatic action forward. Now break the scene into smaller moment-to-moment objectives that serve your major scenic objective. You *always* play an objective, but you can only ever play *one at a time*, although it may — and will — change in an instant as circumstances change during the scene. The point where your objective changes is called a beat; the speed at which this happens is called the transition.

LADY MACBETH'S OBJECTIVE

PATRICK STEWART AND KATE FLEETWOOD IN SHAKESPEARE'S *MACBETH*, THE GIELGUD THEATRE, LONDON, DIRECTED BY RUPERT GOOLD, 2007
In this key scene, Lady Macbeth's scenic objective is to convince the wavering Macbeth that murder is vital and unavoidable.

Choosing your objective

Mark your objectives and the beats in the script and then use the rehearsal and homework to try them out. If some don't work, pick others until they feel right. Choose a want, not a don't want; choose active objectives such as 'I want to make her stay' rather than negative ones like 'I don't want to be rejected.' When choosing your objectives, ask what you could do in a scene rather than what you would do. This is the magic 'what if' of acting. At times your current objective may even contradict your superobjective and your major objective for the scene. Choosing your objectives is the first step. Now you must pursue these objectives through action.

Stay in the moment

Playing an objective happens in the present, so don't anticipate future objectives. Play the current objective until a beat, then switch to the next objective. Play the objective, not the emotion, which should be a natural by-product of the dramatic conflict caused by your wants and obstacles.

Lady Macbeth

Superobjective:
I want to be Queen
I want to rule the world

Scenic objective:
I want to make my husband agree to murder

Moment-to-moment objectives:
To belittle
To mock
To reject
To steel
To emasculate
To make feel guilty
To bully
To shock
To seduce
To sexually arouse

WHAT IS MY OBSTACLE?

The obstacle stands in the way of or opposes what you want. Just as you must always play an action, there is *always* an obstacle, or obstacles. You, the actor, must supply these obstacles to make you pursue your objectives with a sense of immediacy and urgency. Why? Because without obstacles there is no conflict, and consequently no drama. Ask yourself, 'Who and what stops me getting what I want?' in relation to your superobjective, your objective in the scene and your moment-to-moment objectives.

Complex objectives

Your choice of obstacles will influence what you choose to do to overcome them and reach your goal. However, beware of playing the obstacle – you must play your objective in order to overcome your obstacle. Obstacles are not simply objects or people; they can come from your past and present circumstances, your own psyche, the conflicting objectives of other characters, your relationships or surroundings.

A MOTHER'S OBSTACLE

EMMA THOMPSON IN *LOVE ACTUALLY*, DIRECTED BY RICHARD CURTIS, 2003
Thompson's character hides her grief (obstacle) in order to support her children (objective) – despite the realisation of her husband's infidelity.

Interacting with physical objects reinforces your truthful involvement and the way you do this is determined by your wants and obstacles.

AN EXERCISE IN OBSTACLES

Perform a simple task, such as laying a table for important guests. Notice how completely lacking in drama this is. Now repeat, only this time give yourself some obstacles: (time) your guests are arriving in five minutes; (your past) you have never laid table silver service before; (objects) you have hired expensive crockery and will lose a large deposit if there are any breakages; (present circumstances) you don't want to wake your sleeping baby in the corner; (relationship) one of your guests is your hyper-judgmental boss, who will fire you if you mess up; (weather) it's minus four degrees Celsius.

Notice how the obstacles shape and inform the way you perform your task and create conflict within you. The obstacles even conflict with each other, such as the time constraint and the breakages deposit or sleeping baby. In this example, the obstacles force you to work quickly, carefully, quietly. They should make you strive harder to overcome them and, if you leave yourself alone, this conflict will affect you emotionally. You may become flustered, angry, frustrated, despairing, tearful, even hysterical, but those emotions will arise spontaneously from *playing your action*. The emotions were generated organically by the conflict, not because you were pumping to create them.

HOW DO I GET WHAT I WANT?

Acting is *doing* – pursuing your objectives with actions, the things you do, in order to achieve what you want. The things you do can be physical or psychological, but they are always verbs.

Playing with verbs

Once you have decided upon your objectives for a scene, go through the text and write down verbs you will play. Suppose you were trying to borrow a month's wages from your brother to pay off violent creditors. The dialogue might go as below, and some possible actions are in brackets.

STATUS OF POWER

When playing an action, explore what you want to make the other person *feel*.

(I flatter) You're looking really buff – have you been working out? (I impress) Things are going great with me too – (I swagger) I've got a really big deal coming up, but (I level with) here's the thing: (I simper) I need to ask a little favour. (I beg) Please, please, please, will you lend me some money until next Friday? (I cajole) Go on, you know you want to. (I make feel guilty) After all, isn't that what family is for? (I blackmail) If you can't help me, then I may have to tell your wife about you know what ...

Her action here may be 'I compose myself' or 'I shun'. His action appears to be 'I placate' or 'I plead'.

Playing with actions

Your objective is to get your brother to lend you the money, and all your actions – the verbs – pursue this objective. Notice how quickly the actions can change, while the objective stays the same. However, a change of circumstances will cause your objective to change. Suppose your brother suddenly pulls a gun on you – your objective would immediately change to 'I want to escape' or 'I want to kill him' or 'I want to get the gun' (depending on what it says in the script!), and everything you did from then on would pursue this new objective with urgency and immediacy until it changed again. Don't just pursue your actions with your dialogue – you must also use your physicality.

Character and relationships shape actions

We are what we do, so choose your actions based on your character and relationships. In the example we have shown here, the actions reveal your character as manipulative, childish, theatrical, selfish and shallow.

DON'T FORGET THE OBSTACLES

Remember: whatever objective you choose, you must also find the obstacles. So, if your objective is 'I want to escape', your obstacle might be that the door is locked, or he has spiked your drink and your vision is blurred and you feel dizzy. Play an action in spite of these obstacles. Go through your script and delete adjectives from the stage directions. You should not be thinking of doing anything 'angrily' or 'sadly' or 'passionately' — you only play verbs: actions, not emotions.

(I flatter) I walk around my brother staring intently at his musculature, then stand still and nod, then (I impress) adopt a comical He-man pose. (I swagger) I take out a cigar, light it with my ostentatiously expensive lighter then blow a smoke ring. (I level with) I make eye contact and sigh heavily. (I simper) I talk in a baby voice. (I beg) I kneel down and shuffle towards him on my knees, and when I reach him I clasp his hand. (I cajole) I stand up, prod him three times in the ribs with alternating index finger. (I make feel guilty) I walk over to my desk and pick up a family photograph. (I blackmail) I pick up the phone and start dialling his wife's number ...

OBJECTIVES AND ACTION

RICHARD BURTON AND ELIZABETH TAYLOR IN *WHO'S AFRAID OF VIRGINIA WOOLF?* DIRECTED BY MIKE NICHOLS, 1966

George and Martha tear savagely at each other with cutting dialogue — their conflicting wants, and their dysfunctional relationship, make for vital viewing of a relationship in turmoil.

HOW DO I GET WHAT I WANT? | **67**

> We must make this transference, this finding of the characters within ourselves, through a continuing and overlapping series of substitutions from our own experiences and remembrances, and put them in the place of the fiction in the play.
>
> *Uta Hagen*

SUBSTITUTION

The technique of substitution involves replacing people and objects in the play with those from your own life. This helps you to identify with aspects that don't come readily because they are too far from your own experience, and strengthens your sense of involvement and reality. Ideally, by the time you reach the performance, you will have moved beyond the substitution to a point where you identify fully with what your character is experiencing.

SUBSTITUTION IN ACTION

Suppose you were playing a scene in which another character shows you an incriminating letter, which you then have to snatch away in embarrassment. Using substitution, you might make believe that the letter is a photo showing you naked, or a pair of your soiled underpants — anything that makes the moment real and immediate for you.

When should you use substitution?

You will be able to identify with many details of a character's life and circumstances – you have those things 'for nothing' and don't need to work on them, and you may already use substitutions intuitively without realising it. But there will be many aspects that are far away from your life experience and require a substitution to get you there. Only use substitution where identification is difficult.

Helpful substitution

Use substitution of people to reinforce your relationships. If you are supposed to hate, respect, admire, be repulsed by or be deeply in love with the other character, make believe he or she is someone in your real life that makes you feel the same way. You don't have to know them personally – they could be well-known people you have never met. Maybe the action takes place in a beautiful garden, a miserable dungeon or a much-loved family home. Use substitution to bring a garden, hellhole or family home from your real experience into your on-stage life – either with a few details or in its entirety.

RECALLING EMOTION

CHRISTOPHER WALKEN IN *THE DEER HUNTER*, DIRECTED BY MICHAEL CIMINO, 1979
When Walken shot an emotive scene from this film, it is said that he recalled memories from childhood of his parents forcing him to go to summer camp. The experience filled him with abject fear, loss and anger.

ENDOWMENT

Endowment is often confused with substitution, but they are not the same. However, they both stimulate the imagination and use sense memory in order to reinforce on-stage reality. This technique involves endowing the tangible objects you use in your acting with the precise physical qualities that they would have in real life. It isn't always possible to use realistic objects, though – a suitcase may be empty; a knife, blunt; a glass may contain water, which the actor must believe is ice-cold lemonade, gin, hot coffee or bitter hemlock.

Brain imaging technology has shown that thinking about moving a body part triggers the same brain activity as actual movement. Similarly, imagining that a suitcase is heavy triggers a sense memory of how your body should respond.

Draw on your senses

Children are attributed with an instinctive gift for make-believe, but observe a toddler playing with objects and you'll see that they often use them ritualistically or symbolically. The child may put the cup to their lips, and not even drink, or else toss it upwards and glug the contents in an instant, with accompanying slurping noise followed by a satisfied exhale. They don't draw on their sense memory of the weight of the liquid in the cup. There is no testing the heat with the lips before sipping, rising steam touching nose and cheeks, warmth flowing into hands cupped around the mug, the sensation of the hot liquid on the tongue and the back of the throat. *These* are the elements you must experience as an actor, and this technique can't be taught. You develop your physical sense memory by paying attention to how you interact with your physical environment as you go about your daily life. It is make-believe at its simplest, but not in its childish sense.

ENDOWMENT IN ACTION

If the scene requires you to use a priceless, antique heavy necklace, then you would most certainly have to endow it with value and age (tell yourself that it is on loan from the local museum). However, if the prop necklace were plastic or wooden, you would also need to endow its weight, shininess or patina, coolness to touch, musty smell — whatever your reality demands. Use real objects wherever you can, and use endowment only when a necessary element of realism is missing.

Endowing an object can confer both physical qualities and emotional/personal significance.

> ❝ The moment you start playing to the audience you kill any possibility of creating truthful and meaningful action ❞

THE FOURTH WALL

Stage acting demands a peculiar brand of double-thinking – the ability to know that an audience is watching, while at the same time being able to creatively block it out so that it does not intrude on the privacy and reality that you have built up in your imagination and on stage, in order to allow you total creative freedom. The moment you start playing to the audience, you kill any possibility of creating truthful and meaningful action, because you will get caught up in 'entertaining', which inevitably leads to falling back on acting clichés and externals rather than finding the truth of your character in the play from moment to moment.

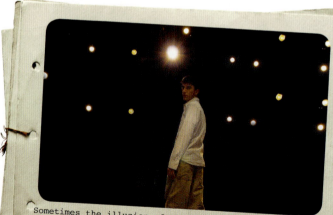

Sometimes the illusion of the Wall is deliberately subverted or discouraged, as with Brecht's *Verfremdungseffekt* – disrupting stage illusion to distance the audience from the action and encourage a more analytical response.

As the other object exercises in this chapter hopefully demonstrate, modern acting is not about playing to the audience (unless you are doing deliberate audience participation). Instead, it is about inviting the audience to observe the specific reality that you and the cast create on stage and believe in fully. Therefore your focus is on what your character wants and does, not on the audience and what you think it likes and wants. Forget the audience! But how? Many actors use a technique called 'the fourth wall'.

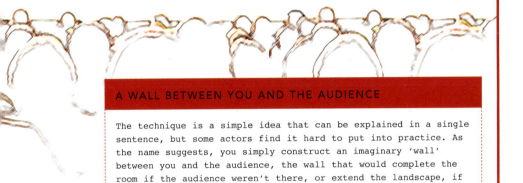

A WALL BETWEEN YOU AND THE AUDIENCE

The technique is a simple idea that can be explained in a single sentence, but some actors find it hard to put into practice. As the name suggests, you simply construct an imaginary 'wall' between you and the audience, the wall that would complete the room if the audience weren't there, or extend the landscape, if the action were set outdoors. You can place imaginary objects on the wall — such as windows, curtains, a fireplace, bookshelves — and any other imaginary objects which help to ground you in the reality of the play.

Don't let it distract

Unless the play or production demands it, don't allow the fourth wall to become primary. For example, there may be a clock on the wall, and your eye may land on it by chance, but if you make a point of deliberately looking at it in order to tell the time, the clock has become primary and a petty distraction from your main purpose on stage. The fourth wall is a construct, a tool – nothing more. Some of your fellow actors will claim to be able to 'see' the fourth wall, finely imagined in every detail. That's great for them, and a sign that they are highly visual people, but don't worry if you can't, and for you the fourth wall is never more than an idea or a metaphor. So long as it performs the function of protecting your reality from being broken by the audience, and preventing you from becoming a performing seal, it has done its job. Move on.

4
CREATING A CHARACTER

Character is revealed by action and, whether you play an emperor or beggar, your main imperative is to be a believable human being. Creating a character starts by reading and re-reading the text and answers the first of the actor's questions: 'Who am I?' Through dynamic research, you build personal connections to magnify qualities within you, and find yourself in a part, psychologically, physically, geographically and socially. You achieve this by discovering everything that made you who you are up until the story begins: the needs and thoughts that drive you to action.

> Ultimately I am just playing myself in different circumstances. So I look for what I might have in common with the character and then take that part of myself and just make it bigger. So it becomes sort of impossible to switch off because it is part of me. So for that period of time that part of me becomes more dominant in my personality.
>
> Michael Sheen

WHO AM I?

It is no accident that 'Who am I?' is the first of the actor's questions (see pages 54–55) because it affects the answers to all the others, and lies at the heart of truthful acting. For example, you can't decide how to pursue a want until you know who you are, because the 'how' is determined by character, relationships and status; you can't give physical expression to your thoughts unless you explore the psychology and physicality of the character; and you won't move beyond a clichéd approach to characterisation until you know who *you* are.

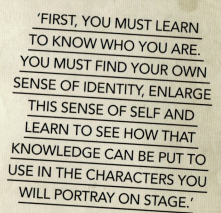

'FIRST, YOU MUST LEARN TO KNOW WHO YOU ARE. YOU MUST FIND YOUR OWN SENSE OF IDENTITY, ENLARGE THIS SENSE OF SELF AND LEARN TO SEE HOW THAT KNOWLEDGE CAN BE PUT TO USE IN THE CHARACTERS YOU WILL PORTRAY ON STAGE.'

UTA HAGEN

Where've you gone?

Actors are often praised for completely 'losing themselves' in a character and their ability to be completely 'taken over' so that their 'real' identity is completely subsumed. This can be quite confusing for the young actor, because it implies a complete disintegration of the self, and it can lead you to strive so hard to lose yourself that you fail to explore you most powerful resource – YOU. Instead of losing yourself, try to find yourself in the part.

'YET CAN I REALLY SAY THAT THAT CREATURE IS NOT PART OF ME? I DERIVED HIM FROM MY OWN NATURE. I DIVIDED MYSELF, AS IT WERE, INTO TWO PERSONALITIES. ONE CONTINUED AS AN ACTOR, THE OTHER WAS AN OBSERVER.'

CONSTANTIN STANISLAVSKI,

BUILDING A CHARACTER

AN OSCAR-WINNING CHARACTERISATION

NICOLE KIDMAN AS VIRGINIA WOOLF IN *THE HOURS*, DIRECTED BY STEPHEN DALDRY, 2002

Kidman's role as the fragile and emotionally unstable Virginia Woolf has gained her critical acclaim. She became almost unrecognisable with her famous prosthetic nose.

TECHNIQUE/MYSTIQUE

In some ways the conflict between technical 'external' acting (where the actor creates an effect) and the more internalised, personalised approach (developed through Stanislavski and the Method, of drawing on your own experiences) is an artificial one. Acting is neither purely technical nor a mystical/psychotic experience — it should probably meet somewhere in the middle. You've got to have the technical discipline and skills, plus the genuine vulnerability, to access and reveal your true emotional responses rather than fake them.

> Whatever you begin with, wherever you put the emphasis, the work must lead you to the action, to the spontaneous doing, giving body and substance to the playwright's and the director's dream, and convincing the audience that this dream is lucid and real.
>
> Uta Hagen

BUILDING A CHARACTER FROM THE TEXT

When you read a play or movie script, for the first time you are the audience and you will respond like the audience; your identification with the plot and the characters within it will be that of an outsider looking in. It is important, when you come to work on the material, that you do not try to recreate the results that the reading first had on you. This will lead you into clichés and chasing after the effect created by your first impressions rather than exploring and building the organic inner life of the character by working through the text.

Who are you?

Before moving on, write a short paragraph that factually describes your character's role and journey through the play. Don't judge or get psychological – think in terms of plot and dramatic conflict. Keep things fluid at this early stage and don't rush into any character decisions. Leave yourself open to a wide range of possibilities while you reread and explore your function and who you are.

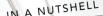

IN A NUTSHELL

As you read and re-read the play, try to define in a sentence what the playwright wants to communicate, so that your character work can build upon his or her intention. This ensures that you always come back to and serve the text, not your own ego. Ask yourself, 'What does the play want?' Only then you can begin the process of exploring the text for clues to your character and background and how your character serves the text.

Serving the text is the only means of developing your character in a meaningful way.

PERSONAL CONNECTIONS

Highlight words and phrases that reveal your role in the play. Identify the human conflicts and opposing needs, because this is what creates the drama, and start to find personal connections, images, smells, sounds and feelings that relate to the events in the script. Write down key words and phrases that inform and describe your character, as you gain a greater understanding of the author's intentions with every reading.

RESEARCH

Research is the process of finding out how your character got to be the way he or she is, physically and emotionally, when the play begins. It starts even before (s)he was born – your parents and the events of their lives affect your own.

Questions, questions, questions!

When and where were you born? What was your childhood like: your key relationships, your education, health, your main drives as a human being? What clothes do you wear? What are your physical characteristics? What is your superobjective (see page 60)? What happened in your past that impinges upon your present and your needs within the play? Don't forget that you know more about the character than (s)he does, so you also need to examine subconscious drives and fears. All the time you are searching for concrete characteristics, events and relationships that enable you to identify with the character's inner life.

If the script is well-known, reading literary criticism has its benefits, but remember that your main priority is to make your character live, rather than get too bogged down by academic interpretations of the text.

'Acting is doing'

All these questions are interrelated and inform each other and impel you to action. There's no point doing all this work if it remains reams of academic analysis that you can't use. You must find a way to take this information to inform your inner life and then use real experiences in your own life, and empathy, to find identification with the character, which translates into needs and action. The character guides you in your actions, and character is expressed through action. As Sanford Meisner never tired of saying, 'Acting is doing.'

CLASSIC CHARACTER CHOICES

JOHN GIELGUD AND ADELE DIXON IN SHAKESPEARE'S
ROMEO AND JULIET, THE OLD VIC, LONDON, DIRECTED BY
HARCOURT WILLIAMS, 1929.

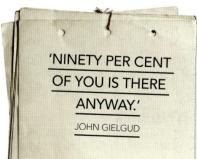

'NINETY PER CENT OF YOU IS THERE ANYWAY.'

JOHN GIELGUD

> For me there always has to be a personal connection, you always look for an area where you and the character meet, where the two cross in some way because that's the way you find something authentic and real.
>
> Ben Whishaw

PHYSICALITY

Stanislavski said that 'The elements of the human soul and the particles of a human body are indivisible', by which he meant that the internal experience of a character and its physical expression are inseparable. If an actor's internal life is genuine, he or she cannot help but find physical expression, so long as his or her body and mind are relaxed and open enough to allow this communication. F. Scott Fitzgerald, and many other writers, have expressed the idea that action is character.

ELEGANCE AND GRACE

AUDREY HEPBURN IN *BREAKFAST AT TIFFANY'S*, DIRECTED BY BLAKE EDWARDS, 1961
Hepburn's waiflike physicality is part of her image as an icon of sophistication and glamour.

From A to somewhere else

Physicality, as it relates to characters, refers to the physical traits specific to the characters you are inhabiting. For example, they may walk in a certain way, stick their chest out, round their shoulders, lead with the nose... Explore the physicality of the character – as revealed by the text – by trying out different ways of speaking, walking and relating to the world around you. Use animal work (see pages 140–143). See how these different physical approaches affect you physiologically, and also how different personality traits inform the physicality.

PHYSICALITY IN ACTION

MARLON BRANDO AND VIVIEN LEIGH IN A *STREETCAR NAMED DESIRE*, DIRECTED BY ELIA KAZAN, 1951
Marlon Brando is at his brooding, masculine best as Stanley Kowalski in the 1951 adaptation of Tennessee William's sexually charged play. His physicality is primal, sensual and brutish. Vivien Leigh also stars, and her physicality is a polar opposite — a delicate fading beauty with constant script references to moths and fragility. Both actors use physicality to perfection in their roles.

GO OFF-ROAD!

Allow yourself to be guided into areas that you wouldn't otherwise have found — that's the creative process. Don't plan to go from A to B, or aim for a preconceived result. Playing around physically will lead you somewhere more interesting altogether.

Making physical connections

Recognise which of your own physical traits you can magnify for the sake of the character and which ones you need to eliminate. Keep exploring and challenging yourself, and don't lock up the character's physicality (or other qualities) too soon. Great actors, like any artists, thrive on the uncertainty of the creative process, so don't lock up your ideas about physicality just to make you feel more comfortable. The worst mistake an actor can make is to create a physicality that allows him or her to make safe acting choices or to hide.

EUREKA!

By remaining open and deepening the connections between your character's inner and physical life, the physical embodiment of the character will seep into you — sometimes gradually, often with a sudden breakthrough, when a specific physical detail opens a window to the complex physical world of the character. This might be through a simple physical activity such as how you brush your teeth or eat an apple, or it could be an item of clothing or personal grooming that either alters your physicality or triggers a 'eureka!' moment.

A simple physical exercise like brushing your teeth or eating an apple in character can unlock your character's inner life.

Intention

Distinguish between the baseline physicality of the character and the physicality that arises from intention. You can perform the same action with limitless different intentions, and the physicality differs each time. For example, imagine walking down the road to post a Christmas card. Now imagine walking down the road to buy a gun to kill your ex-lover. Moment to moment, the physicality changes according to the objective.

The physical properties of personal objects and clothing alter your physicality and help you to make character choices.

'I HAD NO IDEA HOW TO PLAY THE PART… AND THIS MAKE-UP WOMAN, SHE SAID WE'VE GOT TO CUT YOUR HAIR SHORT… THEY WANT US TO PUT A MOUSTACHE ON YOU… I PUT THE MOUSTACHE ON, I LOOKED IN THE MIRROR, I THOUGHT, "THAT'S IT!" SO THE MOUSTACHE PLAYED THE WHOLE PART FOR ME!'

ANTHONY HOPKINS ON DEVELOPING THE CHARACTER OF HENRY WILCOX IN

HOWARDS END

RELATIONSHIPS

Don't be so busy trying to find the character that you neglect one of the most important parts of your character's life – the other people in it, and the corresponding relationships. You must work out your relationship with everyone you meet or even hear about. Our relationship with a person can begin even before we meet them, since we easily build up a mental picture from someone else's description, and they can affect us emotionally without even being present.

Connections

Dorothy and her friends have a relationship with, and expectations about, the Wizard of Oz long before they meet him; indeed, the whole movie depends upon those expectations, and ultimately how they fail to be met. In many ways we are defined by our relationships, and meaning is produced and reproduced through those connections. Therefore fleshing out your relationships with specific details and substitutions (see pages 68–69) that enrich your inner life and affect you emotionally is central to knowing how your character interacts with these other human beings.

Here the actors use substitution to deepen their emotional connection.

FLESH OUT WITH DETAIL

Working on the details of your relationships is not easy — you can do lots of biographical work on paper, but it will only be useful if it becomes actively real to you in performance. Talk to the other actors about your relationships. Do improvisations to explore key scenes and previous circumstances that occur before the play begins, or off-stage during the play to give you a sense memory of the experiences.

Status quo

Work out your *status* in relationship to the characters (see pages 88–89), then start to define your relationship in broad terms – 'I love her', 'I hate him', 'I am frightened of her', 'I feel superior to him', 'I have been betrayed by them'. Then make the details more and more specific, based on the script, and how you want to make the other characters feel. You may love someone but secretly resent them, or you may decide that you hate a person because they subconsciously remind you of yourself (your character might not know this consciously).

Relationships inform how we interact with others and what we try to make them feel.

Major/minor irritants

All this work feeds into your wants and obstacles – and deepens your reality, because drama and conflict are created by relationships. When you get highly specific and detailed, you create a deeply rich inner life that gives you immediacy on stage. For instance, if you decide that the way your lover brushes the hair out of his or her eyes irritates you intensely (assuming it is relevant to the truth of the relationship within the play), every time the other actor does this, they are knowingly or otherwise supplying you with rich input.

STATUS

All human interaction is filtered through the prism of status – each person's real or imagined place in the social hierarchy compared to everyone else. Even in a so-called 'classless' society (if such a thing exists), people make judgements about their own importance in relation to those around them because self-image cannot exist in a vacuum. This is why solitary confinement in prison or on a desert island is such a threat to a person's sense of identity.

It's easily done…

Look around and you will see status at work everywhere – imagine the familiar scene of the snooty hotel receptionist who ingratiates himself to a wealthy guest, only to treat the scruffy guest next in line with thinly disguised contempt. We have status and we play status. The hotel receptionist plays lower status than the wealthy guest because he perceives that part of his job is to make important customers feel pampered (or maybe, as the ultimate snob, he really believes that self-worth is conferred by money), but he then looks down his nose at the scruffy guest because he feels superior (despite the imperative of his job to be welcoming and polite).

Status contrasts are all around us. Observe how people act in different social situations (from a football match to an opera audience).

Physicality v. status

The character you are playing will have an inherent sense of status and your physicality will reflect this. For example – very generally speaking – a high-status character might talk and move slowly and take up a lot of space physically, whereas a person of low status might talk quickly, have nervous movements, take up little space or make expansive gestures to over-compensate. But status also changes during interaction, so when you are rehearsing a scene, try to locate the places where this happens, where one person puts down another or gains the upper hand.

The way we perceive our own status and that of others reveals character and influences our interaction with them.

STATUS IN COMEDY

Comedy is especially reliant on status, and the way it is expressed or undermined, from the basic pratfall to sophisticated status games. Watch any episode of *Fawlty Towers* and you'll see that lots of the humour is underpinned by status – the henpecked husband, the domineering wife, the eager-to-please Spanish waiter, the hotel inspector, the deaf old rich lady. Basil is a man with low self-esteem, who overcompensates by thinking he is better than everyone else, but he is always exposed by his own snobbishness and ensuing loss of status – and therein lies the drama and much of the comedy.

> Vulnerability underlies every human conflict – and thus is at the core of all meaningful acting. Acting that is devoid of genuine vulnerability almost always fails.

Jason Bennett

VULNERABILITY

Great and truthful actors reveal themselves – not just emotionally, but also psychologically. For example, consider that feeling you get when you are lying about something embarrassing, and you know that the other person knows that you are lying. You experience a unique set of physical and emotional responses, specific to you (which is why examples aren't included here, in case you are tempted to copy them instead of recognise your own!). If this situation occurs in performance, you need to find the same responses. This is very revealing and highly personal – you are baring your soul, giving away your secrets (in this example, 'This is what I do when I am lying, everybody!')

Every character has vulnerability which they try to hide, and as an actor you must be prepared to expose your own defence mechanisms by revealing how you behave in given circumstances.

Share your weakness

We all cover up our feelings and use protective strategies. We act all the time to ourselves and to others – to protect us from feeling vulnerable and to prevent others from seeing our weakness – but an actor has to be able to share this quality with an audience above any other. The most technically accomplished and fearless performance won't truly connect unless it allows glimpses of the vulnerability that makes us all human, and this is arguably the greatest risk you can make as an actor.

When you reveal a character's vulnerability you reveal your own, and make a powerful connection with an audience.

'IF YOU'RE GOING TO BE INHIBITED IN FRONT OF EVERYBODY AND NOT DARE TO MAKE A FOOL OF YOURSELF, THEN YOU WILL NEVER GET TO ANYTHING. UNLESS YOU CAN PUSH THE BOAT OUT TOO FAR, THERE'S NO POINT IN CALLING IT BACK.'

JUDI DENCH

> You can play the great roles only if you can compellingly integrate the principles of strength and vulnerability. Antigone speaks and struggles through her tears. Othello and Lear fight and roar like wounded lions even after the full impact of their self-delusions have hit them… Paulina rages at Leontes through a thunderstorm of grief and tears on the seeming death of Hermione.
>
> Robert Castle

Reveal your protective strategies

Good acting means not only accessing this vulnerability, but letting the audience see the strategies you use to cover up your vulnerability in real life. If you can find the courage to share these secrets with the world, you will be a compelling actor, because you will be truthfully human, with all the beauty and ugliness, contradictions and complexity, that this entails. This is a rare commodity indeed, even among some very successful actors. That's the true meaning of vulnerability – not whether you can cry or get angry on cue – just as psychological nakedness is not about taking off all your clothes. If you can make this courageous leap into revealing yourself and your protective strategies, you have at last begun to crack acting.

THE SIX SELVES

In *Creating a Character: A Physical Approach to Acting*, Moni Yakim workshops character through 'six selves [which] embody the most important qualities every actor needs in order to be a well-rounded performer'. They are the *vulnerable* self, the *instinctive* self, the *social* self, the *trusting* self, the *unresolved* self and the *decisive* self. He covers too much to summarise here without being dangerously reductive, but if you can track down a copy, the chapter on the vulnerable self demonstrates very effectively why you should make vulnerability one of your main areas of focus. It contains lots of exercises that help to unlock your vulnerability by magnifying and physicalising perceived personal flaws, so you can be released from their control.

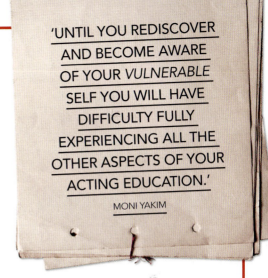

'UNTIL YOU REDISCOVER AND BECOME AWARE OF YOUR *VULNERABLE* SELF YOU WILL HAVE DIFFICULTY FULLY EXPERIENCING ALL THE OTHER ASPECTS OF YOUR ACTING EDUCATION.'

MONI YAKIM

STRENGTH AND WEAKNESS

IAN MCKELLEN IN SHAKESPEARE'S *KING LEAR*, COURTYARD THEATRE, STRATFORD-UPON-AVON, DIRECTED BY TREVOR NUNN, 2007.

IMPROVISATION

No book on acting would be complete without a section on improvisation, which is one of the best ways to free the body, mind and imagination, and extend your sense of fun, spontaneity and observational and listening skills. It is also a means to explore character and develop scenes. However, of all the techniques and challenges that acting offers, improvisation is most definitely something you cannot learn from a book (which is probably why there are only a handful on the subject, including the seminal *Improvisation* by John Hodgson and Ernest Richards).

Improvisation is a constant reminder that acting is a collaborative process.

Lie back, and…

In his introductory class in week one of drama training at the Royal Academy of Dramatic Art (RADA), improvisation pioneer and teacher Ben Benison used to get the entire class of first-year students to lie flat on their backs on the floor. And there they stayed for three hours. Nothing was planned, but plenty happened. Unsure what they were supposed to be doing, lying immobile in silence, punctuated by the occasional comment or random noise from Ben, after about 20 minutes a ripple of infectious laughter would usually spread around the room. Some students resisted and got angry, thinking they were wasting their time, since 'nothing' was happening. But those who allowed themselves to engage with this beguilingly simple non-exercise discovered that something wonderful and life-affirming and unexpected and crazy and infuriating and spontaneous can take you over, fill you with pleasure and brush away your preconceptions and taboos if you just open yourself up, put aside your judgements, and have fun, in the moment. What a wonderful introduction to the joy of acting!

JUST IMPROV IT!

There are myriad approaches to improvisation and, while it is essential for an actor's development, you can only learn it by *doing*. So, sign up for some improv classes, break some rules and enjoy working beyond your comfort zone.

Improvisation develops essential acting skills like listening, being in-the-moment, risk-taking and resisting the urge to self-censor.

"Ben sort of taught me to be fearless, really, and to take risks and not to be afraid of looking stupid and making mistakes and being spontaneous and not being too bogged down, because on the one hand we'd have acting classes that were very kind of Method-based, very structured and I guess there were a lot of rules to it. And then in Ben's classes you'd just have to break all the rules and not be frightened.

Michael Sheen

5
THE VOICE

This chapter introduces the importance of vocal training and daily practice to increase range and responsiveness, as this is the only way to achieve your expressive potential and find the essential truth of your own authentic voice. Vocal training teaches you to support the breath and to utilise all the resonating spaces in your head and body. It also develops the strength and flexibility of the muscles involved in speech production, and increases clarity of speech, range and power so that your voice is fully available to communicate your imagination and intention.

> # The three most important things for an actor are voice, voice and yet again, voice.
>
> Constantin Stanislavski

WHY TRAIN THE VOICE?

The voice is intimately associated with identity and self-expression, which is why it can be a sensitive area for training, but there is no escaping the reality that actors must develop their voices to communicate their intentions effectively.

MUSCLE WORKOUT

Training the voice should never be just a bunch of physical exercises to improve vocal agility, nor is it learning how to talk 'correctly'. Vocal training teaches you to relax and breathe from the diaphragm at the base of the ribs to bring into play the various resonating spaces in your head and body. It also develops the strength and flexibility of the muscles used in speech production. Ultimately it allows you to respond instinctively, so that you move beyond trying to create a pleasing or powerful sound to expressing your intentions with clarity, range and power.

Breathing from the diaphragm and grounding the breath is the founda[tion] for the rest of your vocal techni[que]

Vocal training

Vocal training teaches you how to increase the range and responsiveness of your voice; it is a process of creative self-development to uncover the essential truth of your voice, to explore its possibilities and develop freedom and flexibility. When a voice teacher emphasises the importance of 'Received Pronunciation' (standard pronunciation of British English), some actors, especially those with regional accents, become defensive about losing part of their identity, and with good reason. However, vocal training is so much more than this. It allows you to find your own authentic voice, because our preconceptions, sense of identity and how we think we sound often stop us from achieving our expressive potential.

DAILY REGIME

The tensions and restrictions that you place upon yourself as an actor lock up the body, the breathing and the voice. Vocal development addresses these limitations so it can transform your entire creative process. For example, if you have a tendency to push and over-explain to an audience, or over-energise, these drives will affect your voice in specific ways (neck tension, too much head tone, using too much breath, being too loud). Therefore a daily programme that challenges you vocally and imaginatively can be the key to recognising and freeing up the core creative blocks that diminish your effectiveness as an actor.

Vocal training teaches you to support the breath and connect it to thoughts and emotions.

THE MECHANISM OF SOUND PRODUCTION

The breath hits the vocal cords while they are drawn together, causing them to vibrate and make sound waves. These waves are amplified as they resonate through the head and body. You use your lips, teeth and palate to change the sound into words. The sound travels from your body to the listener's ear, but on the way it is further influenced by the acoustics of the environment.

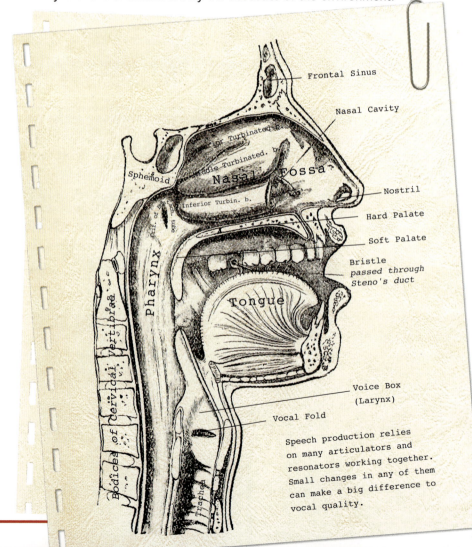

Speech production relies on many articulators and resonators working together. Small changes in any of them can make a big difference to vocal quality.

Resonators

The quality of the sound you produce depends on your individual physical make-up, but also on the body's resonators. You have various resonators in your body – the chest, mouth, nose, the pharynx (the back of the throat immediately behind the tongue, above the larynx), nasal cavities, sinuses and facial bones. The quality of the voice depends on which areas of the body contribute most to the resonance. For example, people with thin nasal voices focus their energy in the nose and nasal cavity, while 'plummy' voices are due to an excess of pharangeal resonance.

Chest resonance

As an actor you need to become aware of how to combine different resonators, and especially to develop your chest resonance so that your vocal tone is rich. You must become more aware of how you are using your voice so that it is available to express the full range of your character's emotional life, but not get caught up in how you sound – otherwise, you will draw the audience's attention to you the actor, rather than the character you are playing.

RESONATING THE BODY CAVATIES EXERCISE

Place your hand just below the solar plexus. Gently hum. Allow the sound to vibrate in this area for one minute. Then, place your hand onto your upper chest. Gently hum. Allow the vibration to fill this area for a further minute. It should feel like a very light internal massage. The vibrating skin may itch.

ALIGN YOUR BODY

You develop chest resonance by proper alignment and use of the body, by using a system such as the Alexander Technique (see page 128) and then rooting the breath (see page 102). You must also eliminate tension in the jaw (see page 107), increase the muscularity of tongue and lips (see pages 110—111) and then assimilate this new way of working such that you can put all this together and respond to the instinct of the moment. It's quite a challenge, but stick with it. When you start training the voice, some exercises have startling results — tapping into chest resonance for the first time can be a revelation, but these fleeting breakthroughs must be supported by a routine of daily work. Whenever you work with a vocal coach, or do vocal exercises at home, always try to deepen your understanding of *why* you are doing a particular exercise, and then you'll be motivated to put in the required training.

RELAXATION AND BREATHING

In daily life most of us are accustomed to breathing from the upper part of the chest – especially when exercising, when we need to take short breaths to deliver oxygen to our muscles quickly. However, this creates a lot of tension in the ribs and shoulders, and is inappropriate for the actor who needs an upper body free to resonate and amplify the sound made when the breath passes through the vocal cords. Most important of all, you can only make an emotional connection with the breath when it is rooted in your lower abdomen and back.

Rooting the voice

Lie on your back, with your bare feet flat on the floor, knees slightly apart, bent and pointing to the ceiling. You may prefer to rest your head on a book (about 2 cm thick) so that your neck is aligned with your spine. Make sure all your back is in contact with the floor, especially the lower back, but don't force it by pressing your body into the floor. If there is a slight arch there, your back should spread and make better contact as you become more relaxed. Your arms can rest by your side, or you can place your hands on your abdomen, with your elbows resting on the floor. Allow your back to lengthen and your shoulders to widen. Don't do anything: just send the order with your thoughts and the muscles will respond. Gently rotate your head from side to side if it feels tense, shake your hands a little, and then let them drop. Spend a few minutes in this 'semi-supine' position, and enjoy feeling supported by the floor.

The 'semi-supine' position comes from yoga, where it is used to align and lengthen the spine and allow the back to spread. Maintain awareness as you relax.

Remaining in the 'semi-supine' position, try another exercise working with your breath. While keeping your shoulders and upper chest relaxed, with the waist and stomach muscles pulled in towards the spine, place one hand on the navel and the other on the upper chest. Take a breath in and out, trying not to allow either of the hands to rise or fall. All the movement should happen from the lower ribs only. Repeat 10 times, gradually deepening the breath each time. This next exercise uses the body's natural reflex system to ensure that your breathing remains powerful without building any unnecessary pressure — it is important at the early stages of breathing work not to hold your breath when the lungs are full. This creates tension and pressure in the throat preventing it from remaining open and relaxed.

Focus on your breathing

Place the backs of your hands at the bottom of your ribcage so you can feel the expansion and contraction of your lower back as you breathe in and out. Breathe in slowly through your nose and then sigh noiselessly (ie, don't engage your vocal cords) as you exhale, expelling all the air. Release the stomach muscles and take another breath through your nose. Continue to breathe in and out, and feel the ribs and the sides of your back responding. Keep your upper chest relaxed, but don't involve it in your breathing – you should by now be aware that the movement is coming from the bottom of your ribs.

By placing your hands on your ribcage and exhaling with your mouth open, you can feel how the ribs expand and contract as you breathe.

Control the outgoing breath

Now that you have centred your breath, you can control it as you exhale. Breathe in again slowly, then breathe out to a slow count of ten (in your head). If you hear a rasping sound of air, it means that you are holding tension in your neck and jaw. Your throat should be open. If at any point you feel like yawning, let it happen, as it is a good way to release tension and open the throat. Always expel all the air, and pause for a moment before you inhale, so you can become familiar with the sensation of your abdominal muscles springing back automatically to allow the breath to flow in. You don't have to force it.

Yoga can give you a better awareness of the relationship between breath and the body as well as helping you with posture and flexibility.

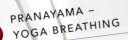

PRANAYAMA – YOGA BREATHING

Yoga breathing, or Pranayama, is the science of breath control. It consists of series of exercises especially intended to meet the body's needs and keep it in vibrant health. Pranayama comes from three words in Sanskrit; Prana, meaning 'life force' or 'life energy', Yama, meaning 'discipline' or 'control', and Ayama meaning 'expansion', 'non-restraint' or 'extension'.

Exercise your diaphragm

Remaining on the floor, you can now exercise the diaphragm by placing your palms on your abdomen and giving several little pants as your exhale ('huh') until you are confident that the sound is springing from the diaphragm, rather than being pushed out of the upper chest or throat. You can even speak some lines of text, and notice how effortlessly you can speak when your breath is rooted, and your throat free from tension. You should also notice that your speaking voice sounds more resonant – but more importantly, it feels more available to you.

Remaining in the 'semi-supine' position, you will notice a greater resonance in your voice as the breath becomes rooted.

CLARITY OF SPEECH

There is no 'right' way of speaking, but there is a tangible difference between clear and unclear speech. Clarity comes from linking your vocal energy with the intention of the word and by freeing the jaw and finding the correct amount of energy in the muscles of the tongue, lips and soft palate. These ingredients are vital for the production of vowels and consonants.

VOWELS AND CONSONANTS

Vowels are shaped by the lips and tongue, and are formed by the free passage of vocalised sound. Consonants are formed by initially blocking the sound and then releasing suddenly on the plosive consonants 'p' and 'b', gradually on 'n' and 'l', and more gradually still with 's' and 'z', where the sound is channelled down the middle of the tongue. Precision is important, because a small movement or placement of the tongue, lips or palate can make a big difference to the sound. This is why actors do exercises that focus on each vowel and consonant separately, so they work individual muscles, and learn to use the requisite amount of energy for each.

Vocal training reduces vocal strain and ensures you do not damage your vocal cords.

WAKE-UP WARM-UP

Begin with this short warm-up to energise and stretch. Stand comfortably with your legs shoulder width apart. Allow your head to drop your head forward so that your chin is close to your chest (don't press it down). Roll your head slowly round in a circle two or three times, then reverse the direction and repeat. Bring your head back up. Chew with exaggerated facial movement — involve all of your face. Take a deep breath and blow your lips out like a horse, three times. Massage your face. Rub your ears. Pull your earlobes, and stroke your hands down your jaw. Stick your tongue out as far forward as it will go, then draw a big circle, and change direction. Point the tongue tip to your nose, then to your chin, then left and right.

Begin every vocal session by warming up and waking up your face.

Release the jaw

In cold climates the jaw is tight and the teeth are closed, whereas in warmer climates the jaw is more relaxed and fluid, and everyone lies somewhere on this spectrum. Actors need a free jaw; otherwise, both resonance and articulation are affected. Correct alignment of the head and neck (see Alexander Technique, pages 128–129) will release a stiff jaw over time, but if you are aware of tension in your jaw (maybe you have been chewing gum, or clenching your teeth as a stress response) you should open your mouth, letting your jaw float free, and gently stroke your closed fingers down either side of the jawline. Massaging the ears also helps – rubbing briskly, pulling the earlobes and paying special attention to the point where the jaw articulates with the skull.

TONGUE-TIP EXERCISES

We recommend you read *Voice and the Actor*, which is a classic work by Cicely Berry, world-renowned voice director of Britain's Royal Shakespeare Company. She details scores of vocal exercises, but on the following pages are four exercises to start you off with the consonants 't', 'd', 'n' and 'l'. The tongue needs to be flexible and responsive, and you may be tempted to think that you get enough exercise from speaking, but it is important to isolate the sounds, so you can work on precision without tensing the jaw.

CLARITY OF SPEECH | 107

L IS FOR LAH

This 'L' exercise makes you focus on accurate placement of the tongue tip and the correct use of breath energy.

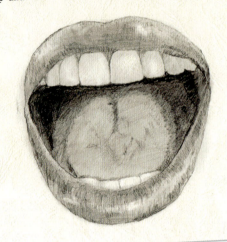

L

Open your mouth to the width of two fingers, but don't force it. Now say 'lah' and be aware of the pressure of the tongue tip behind the teeth while you trap the sound and then release into the vowel. At the end of the 'lah', your tongue tip should finish up resting behind your bottom teeth. Repeat a few times, then increase the number of syllables to 'lahlahlahlaaaah' and speed up, while maintaining and observing the firm and accurate placement of the tongue tip. Keep the jaw free and the back of the tongue relaxed, *and make the tongue tip do all the work.*

Here the actress is stretching the tongue, but when she articulates, her tongue tip should be precise and nimble, while the back of the tongue stays relaxed.

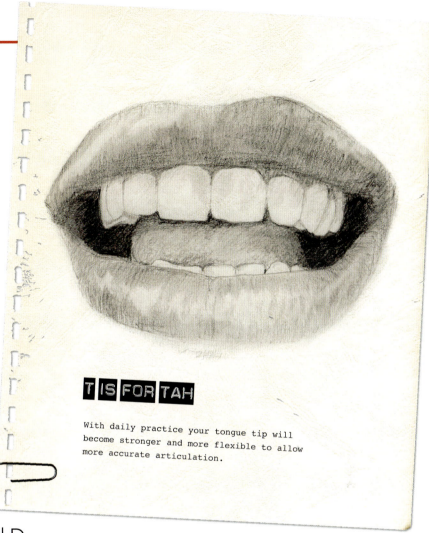

T IS FOR TAH

With daily practice your tongue tip will become stronger and more flexible to allow more accurate articulation.

T and D

Say 'tah'. The consonant is formed by placing the tongue tip on the ridge behind the top front teeth, closing off the sound momentarily until you release into the vowel. There should be no escape of air until then (if this happens, it's a sign that your tongue tip needs strengthening and using with more precision). Repeat a few times, then increase the number of syllables to 'tahtahtahtaaaah' and speed up, while maintaining and observing the firm and accurate placement of the tongue tip. Keep the jaw free and the back of the tongue relaxed, and, once again, *make the tongue tip do all the work*. Repeat with D.

N

'Nah' is formed by lowering the soft palate so that resonance is created in the nose. However, you should pay attention to the dexterity and firm muscularity of the tongue tip, as before; otherwise, you will create a nasal sound, since the air must escape through the mouth when you release into the vowel. Increase the number of syllables to 'nahnahnahnaaaah' and pick up the speed. Don't move your jaw as you speed up – focus on keeping the back of the neck and jaw free and the back of the tongue relaxed.

'THE VOICE WILL NEVER BE AS GOOD IN EXERCISE AS IT WILL BE WHEN YOU HAVE DONE THE EXERCISES, FORGOTTEN THEM, AND ARE USING THE VOICE IMAGINATIVELY.'

CICELY BERRY, VOICE AND THE ACTOR

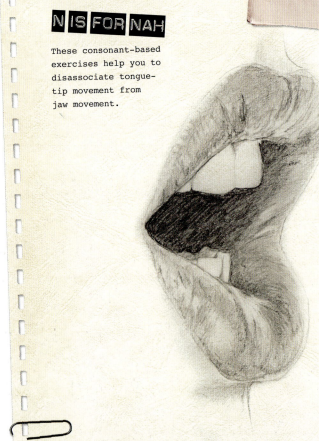

N IS FOR NAH

These consonant-based exercises help you to disassociate tongue-tip movement from jaw movement.

DIALOGUE COACH

THE ORIGINAL POSTER FROM *BEAUTÉ VOLÉE* (STEALING BEAUTY), DIRECTED BY BERNARDO BERTOLUCCI, 1996

Cicely Berry, voice director of the Royal Shakespeare Company and world-renowned for her work as a voice and text coach, worked as dialogue coach on this film drama. The film is primarily in the English language, but Italian, French, Spanish and German are also spoken by several of the characters through the course of the film.

> From the very beginning you must start to use the voice on material that will stretch it, material that can be used over and over again because it is possible to get different things out of it each time.
>
> Cicely Berry, *Voice and the Actor*

SMELL THE ROSE

Once the breath is rooted in your lower abdomen and back, 'smelling the rose' can help you to make an emotional connection with your breathing, as well as teach you to experience an energy that invites an audience to share, rather than to push out sound to reach them.

As described in step 2, allow yourself to relax in a back bend.

1. Stand with your legs shoulder width apart, knees not bent, but not locked straight (they should be comfortable and relaxed).

2. Starting with your head, curl down your spine so that you end up flopping over with your fingers touching the floor (or hanging, if you can't reach the floor), head loose, with the top of your head facing the floor. Your legs are still straight, but relaxed, so that you are bent over at the waist. Shake your shoulders very gently to help you loosen up. Remain in this position for a few minutes, allowing your spine to lengthen. Don't push – relax, go floppy and don't lock your knees.

3. Breathe deeply – in through the nose, feeling the air fill your lower abdomen and lower back, then out through your mouth with a sigh. Keep going until you are sure that the breath is rooted.

4. Curl up to standing position, starting with your coccyx and ending with your head. Stand upright and, while your feet support you firmly on the floor, imagine that there is a string on the top of your head that is pulling you upwards.

5. Place one hand on your stomach and hold an imaginary rose in front of your face with the other. Breathe in through your nose, and use your sense memory to fill up your senses with the sweet fragrance. Let it beguile your sinuses and facial cavities, awaken your face and take life in your whole body. Breathe in the delicate scent right down to your abdomen. Feel the pleasure in your belly as you exhale and say, 'Yummy yummy yummy yummy yummy', keeping your lips expressive and your throat free. Remain active in the eyes, mouth and face (don't zone out). Enjoy the feeling of buoyancy in your lower back and front of the pelvis. The words originate from the pleasurable feeling in your belly, but the sense of vocal effort is focused behind the nose and above the soft palate rather than at the front of the vocal tract. You don't send the sound out. It lives and resonates like a ball of energy living in the perfumed arch behind your face.

The pleasant fragrance fills the diaphragm with a buoyant energy, connected to an emotional response.

> The clear way through to the meaning of a piece is not all by trying to make the most of every word.

Peter Barkworth

SINGING

Singing your way through a piece of text is a great way to free the voice and open up new possibilities of rhythm and range. You can either chant on one note, or make up a tune, allowing your musical phrasing to be led by the meaning. Extend the vowels so that you are required to use more breath and power to communicate. Classically trained singers use this process in reverse when they want to explore singing in a more contemporary style. They might take a few lines of a song and speak them as if they are talking to a close friend on the phone.

Be brave and have fun with your voice — singing the script is a great way to discover new meaning and phrasing.

Sing the text

Singing the text and creating an uninterrupted sound can help you to discover the thoughts and emotions that lie behind the music of the text, because you will naturally open up possibilities. When you return to speaking the lines, you will be more aware of the momentum of the thought, the rhythm of the language, as well as the amount of range that is available to you. Sometimes the desire to be 'truthful' can lead you to restrict your vocal range, or lock up the sound inside you, but singing the text removes these blocks.

Speak loud and high

After you have sung the text, rather than going straight back to the naturalistic spoken word, try speaking the text loudly and at a much higher pitch than your normal speaking range, while keeping the breath rooted in the diaphragm. Then bring the pitch down gradually to reach your middle voice so you can feel the chest resonances but still keep some high notes. We all use a wide range of inflections in our daily conversation. However, actors often limit their range by getting caught up in the words and the sounds they are producing, rather than the involvement of the conviction of the thoughts generating the impulse for the breath and the words.

Opera singers will use this technique in another way, speaking the lines to explore language outside the confines of the melodic structure.

GETTING PHYSICAL

Actors can feel very apprehensive when faced with 'important' text, whether it is a Shakespearean sonnet or a famous scene from *Cat on a Hot Tin Roof*. Some actors become overly reverent and tie themselves up in classical knots, while others over-compensate by ignoring the form and become too naturalistic. Exploring the material physically – especially poetry – breaks down the mystique and gives you the freedom to experiment and stake out your own territory.

Get moving

When you are exploring language and your voice, take every opportunity to get physical with it. Running round the room, jumping, skipping, rolling around on your back, climbing, digging, punching and throwing a ball are just some of the ways that you can free up the voice by using your body. This physical activity opens you up and stops you getting locked into habitual thought patterns or preconceptions about how your voice should sound, or how a piece of text should be approached.

PLAY AROUND

You must give physical
expression to your ideas;
otherwise, if you do all
your textual homework
sitting in a chair, you will
self-censor. Many of your
best ideas will live and die
in your head and never find
expression. So, always
explore imaginative ways to
play with the thoughts,
words, sounds and rhythms
by using your body. You
don't have to give the
definitive performance, or
say, 'This is what it
means', or tell everyone
everything you know.

Play around with extremes of movement. It is
better to tone down after a discovery than
miss opportunities by playing it safe.

GETTING PHYSICAL | **117**

6
MOVEMENT

THE ACTOR'S BODY

Actors must be able to use their bodies with physical and emotional confidence and efficiency. They should also be fit, possess strength and stamina and be flexible and free from unwanted tension so that they are open to respond to the physical and emotional demands of any part.

Developing your body's flexibility and your awareness of areas of tension improves general fitness and well-being, and reduces the risk of injury.

PURSUING A WANT

Actors are often let down by their inability to marry their inner life with their external movement, and many never move beyond this point. However, Method acting teaches you that your entire being, mind and body should always be engaged in pursuing the character's wants moment by moment through action (which is not the same thing as movement). Unless you understand this concept, any theories of movement or physical training you undertake to increase your fitness or flexibility or unlock your emotions will just be add-ons that you will bolt onto this flawed understanding. You will never feel comfortable in your body and will inevitably fall back on hollow stage gestures or vague unfocused movement that is disconnected from your character's inner life.

Flexibility and being aware of your own body's boundaries are vital to a long and varied acting career.

Movement

Being disconnected from your character isn't helped by drama training that tends to compartmentalise movement, voice, text, Method classes, etc. Your internal impulses arise through the wants of your character – so if you are truly focused and involved in pursuing these wants, your internal impulses will naturally and truthfully give rise to action and physical movement because there is no other way for you to pursue these wants. Movement training makes your body available so that it can respond instinctively to these drives (animal work is a good way to experience this; see pages 140–143). That does not mean that you cannot access your inner life from the physical. The physical approach to acting can unlock all sorts of sense memories and emotions, as Grotowski's *Exercises Plastiques* demonstrate (see pages 144–147).

THE IMPULSE TO MOVEMENT

You may become an expert at yoga or Alexander Technique, unlock the resonant and expressive potential of your voice, you may identify and correct the habitual ways you use your body inappropriately, you may identify various emotional restrictions in your personality and how they create the various physical blocks in your body, you may be able to backflip off a wall or sword fight without breaking a sweat — but all this will be indulgent self-exploration unless you understand that the impulse to movement and how you use your body always comes back to what your character wants. Remember this as you work to increase your body awareness.

FLEXIBILITY AND PLASTICITY OF MOTION

Young actors often have difficulty understanding why they have to spend so much of their training developing their flexibility. If you go to any drama school, you'll spend hour upon hour rolling around on your back, doing cat stretches, giving each other full-body massages and a whole heap of other physical exercises that may seem to some to be far removed

from the business of acting. However, unless you want to limit your range to playing muscle-bound action heroes, developing flexibility and plasticity of motion is vital to a long and varied career. You will no doubt be familiar with the idea that stretching exercises develop flexibility, but there are several basic types of stretching, and not all of them are suitable for you.

Many actors start out with visible amounts of tension in the neck and shoulders. This restricts the movement of the jaw, affecting speech, as well as causing tension in the rest of the body.

A flexible body connects fluidly to
the senses and is more responsive in
the living moment.

Ballistic stretching

This involves using the momentum of a stretched limb or body part to force it beyond its natural range. This type of stretching is very frequent in sport, such as bouncing down to touch your toes. Ballistics often uses jerky movements, which can lead to injury and is unsuitable for everyone including sportspeople. Avoid ballistic stretching, but it is OK to use bouncing motions to release tension so long as they don't involve a stretch, eg, bouncing your shoulders gently up and down.

FLEXIBILITY PROS

On a purely practical level, being flexible makes you less prone to injury, and allows you to use your body more efficiently, so you'll also have greater stamina. Also, it looks better. No-one likes to see a stiff actor perform. People want to see expressive bodies that are available to express the full range of emotional and physical demands that playing a part fully requires. An inflexible body is sometimes a symptom of an inflexible mind.

Dynamic stretching

This involves slow, controlled movements through the full range of motion, as well as increasing the range and/or speed of motion gradually, smoothly and gently. Dynamic stretching is great for warming up, while static stretches are best for cooling down after exercise. Here are some examples of dynamic stretching.

Using a 'hula hoop' when doing your hip circles is a fun way of turning this into cardio-active activity.

STRETCH YOURSELF...

- Joint rotations: stand with your legs shoulder width apart, hands hanging freely by your side. Flex, extend and rotate each of these joints in turn: finger, wrist, elbow, shoulders, neck, hips, knees, ankles, feet, toes.
- Lateral neck stretch: gently and slowly move your right ear towards your right shoulder, then lower your left ear towards your left shoulder. Exhale into the stretch. Repeat five times.
- Shoulder circles: raise your right shoulder towards your right ear, take it backwards, down and then up again to the ear in a smooth action. Repeat with the other shoulder.

... AND SOME MORE!

- **Hip circles:** With hands on your hips, and feet spread wider than the shoulders, make circles with your hips in a clockwise direction for 10 to 12 repetitions. Then repeat in an anticlockwise direction.
- Raise your right arm above your head. Try to touch the ceiling with your palm, at the same time stretching your left arm down the left leg with fingers pointing to the floor.
- **Half squat:** Hold your hands out in front. From a standing position, with your feet flat on the floor, bend at the knees smoothly as you breathe out. Keep your back straight, and knees pointing over your toes, until your thighs are parallel to the floor. Then straighten your legs as you breathe in and return to standing. Repeat 12 times.

It is important you continue
to breathe deeply throughout
so that your muscles relax
into the stretches.

Active stretching

Also known as static-active stretching, this involves getting your body into a stretch, and then maintaining this position using the relevant agonist muscles (see below). An example of an active stretch is extending and raising your leg sideways and holding it in this position using your leg muscles.

Passive stretching

This is when you adopt a position and use apparatus or another body part to help you maintain the position. If you extend and raise your leg sideways and then hold it in position with your hand, this is a passive stretch. Passive stretching is good for cooling down after exercise.

Isometric stretching

This passive stretch (the splits) can be adapted into an isometric stretch by tensing the thighs during the position for 7–15 seconds before relaxing.

Isometric stretching is static – it doesn't use motion. Instead, it involves subjecting a muscle that is already stretched to an isometric contraction in order to stretch muscle fibres that would otherwise remain relaxed. The joint angle and muscle length do not change, hence the name: *iso* (same) *metric* (distance). The benefit is that you can stretch without weakening the joints, but it is a very powerful form of stretching, and therefore not recommended for anyone under 18. It also actually strengthens tendons and ligaments, while maintaining their flexibility, whereas traditional static stretching pulls the fibres apart (which can lead to joint instability).

AN ISOMETRIC STRETCH

Place your outstretched leg on a chair, with toes pointing upwards. Now lean forward and use your body weight to stretch your hamstrings. This is a traditional static stretch. In this position, if you then press your heel into the chair (ie, attempt to bend your knee) this become an isometric stretch. Your hamstring will try to contract, but it won't be able to because of the stretch, so the fibres are being pulled from both sides. This will not only increase flexibility in the hamstring but also strengthen the muscle in this position, which makes it capable of withstanding more force, and therefore preventing injury.

MUSCLES IN AN ACTIVE STRETCH

Most muscles of the musculoskeletal system work in pairs — agonists and antagonists. When you move a body part, the muscle responsible for the motion, the agonist, contracts or shortens. At the same time, the corresponding antagonist muscle stretches. When the body part returns to its starting position, the reverse happens. For example, when you perform a dumbbell curl, the bicep (agonist) contracts as you lift the weight upwards, while the tricep (antagonist) stretches. When you lower the weight, the bicep (now the antagonist) relaxes and stretches, while the tricep (now the agonist) does the contracting. Most yoga positions involve active stretching.

This yoga position, called 'warrior two', employs active stretching.

ALEXANDER TECHNIQUE

Acting places great demands on the mind and the body, but even in daily life we all build up unwanted muscle tension and develop a repertoire of usually subconscious physical habits that lock up the mind, body, emotions, breathing and the voice, all of which ultimately block creative expression, leading to even greater tension.

Re-educate mind and body

Alexander Technique involves re-educating the mind to allow the body to perform with maximum efficiency, and therefore improves posture and muscle tone. It brings greater awareness of how you use your body, which is why it underpins acting training in many of the world's top drama schools. The technique was devised by a nineteenth-century actor named Frederick Matthias, who wanted to understand why he kept losing his voice. Matthias discovered that he pulled his head back and downwards before delivering his lines. This compressed his spine and ribs, hampered his breathing and placed incredible strain on his voice.

An Alexander Technique practitioner will be able to guide you towards the most efficient use of your body. Be warned, it may feel odd at first

Life-changing

The Alexander Technique is an 'active' therapy – one could even say philosophy – since its principles can be applied to every aspect of your life. It begins by saying 'No' to habitual thought processes, so that you can allow a better mental and physical experience to unfold. It is very much about focusing on the now rather than 'end-gaining', by actively striving to rid yourself of tension, which just leads to more tension…

CONFUSED? INTRIGUED?

Like most therapies or philosophies, Alexander Technique is devilishly simple. Yet you could spend a lifetime exploring it to deepen your understanding of your mind and body. There are many books on the subject, but the only way to experience it correctly is to have at least 20 lessons with an Alexander Technique practitioner. They will gently manipulate your body and guide you through the system.

HABITUAL PHYSICALITY

A good example of habitual physicality is the simple act of getting out of a chair, when many people raise their head backward, lift their shoulders and lead with their chin (try it now and see what you do). But there is a better way: using Alexander Technique, crudely speaking, you would lead with the top of your head according to the mantra: 'Neck free. Head forward and up. Back lengthen. Back widen. Legs forward and away.'

THE MANTRA

NECK FREE.
HEAD FORWARD AND UP.
BACK LENGTHEN.
BACK WIDEN.
LEGS FORWARD AND AWAY.

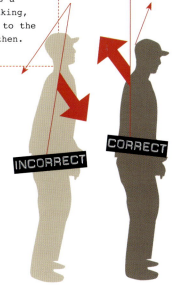

INCORRECT

CORRECT

LABAN MOVEMENT THEORY

Laban Movement Theory is a system of studying the mechanics of human movement, and was devised by Rudolf Laban (1879–1958). His work has provided the foundations of modern dance and is a useful tool for the actor, because it breaks down movement into four Motion Factors: Space, Time, Weight and Flow.

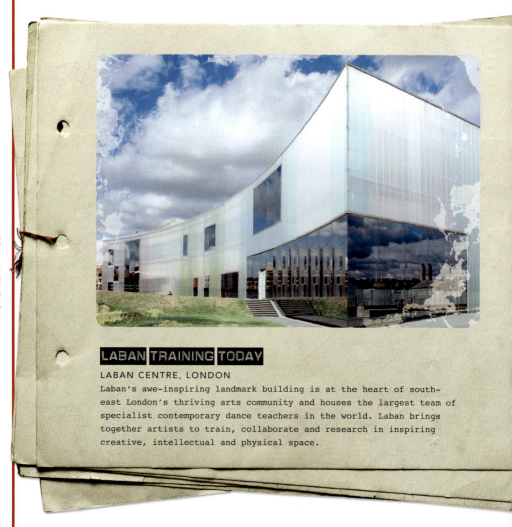

LABAN TRAINING TODAY

LABAN CENTRE, LONDON

Laban's awe-inspiring landmark building is at the heart of south-east London's thriving arts community and houses the largest team of specialist contemporary dance teachers in the world. Laban brings together artists to train, collaborate and research in inspiring creative, intellectual and physical space.

Endless possibilities

This detailed analysis of movement helps you to explore more possibilities both in terms of making character choices and pursuing your character's wants. It's another way of making you focus on the details of movement and gestures available to you and opens up more choices. It can also can be a good way to explore how changing the way you use your body generates different emotional responses – the body affecting the emotions, rather than the other way around.

THE MOTION FACTORS

- Space relates to the direction of the movement (up, down, left, right, forwards, back) and is linked with *thinking*, *attention* and *orientation*.
- Time relates to speed of movement and is connected to ideas such as *intuition* and *rhythm*.
- Weight is the muscular energy or force used in the resistance to weight (ie, gravity). It also relates to *sensing* and *intentionality*.
- Flow is connected to the feeling, and *progression*, of the motion, and ranges on a scale from '*bound*' to '*free*'.

Body and emotions in synch

We have seen in earlier chapters that emotions spring naturally through pursuing your character's objective, but it is also useful to explore how your emotions can be affected by manipulating the body. Here's a very crude example. If you collapse your chest and look at the floor, you may start to feel sad, depressed, weak, hopeless and low-status, whereas if you fling open your arms and look at the sky, you may feel happy, strong, hopeful and important.

Flinging your hands up into the sky creates different emotions from collapsing your chest or hugging your knees.

The kinesphere

Laban was also interested in the kinesphere, the personal space within our reach. It is like a large bubble that we inhabit, and moves with us wherever we go. Sometimes our kinesphere overlaps with those of other people.

EFFORT ACTIONS

Laban also categorised eight 'Effort Actions' by combining the first three Motion Factors:
• press (direct, sustained, strong)
• wring (indirect, sustained, strong)
• glide (direct, sustained, light)
• float (indirect, sustained, light)
• thrust (direct, sudden, strong)
• slash (indirect, sudden, strong)
• dab (direct, sudden, light)
• flick (indirect, sudden, light)

BALLET DIRECTOR

TCHAIKOVSKY'S *SLEEPING BEAUTY*, DIRECTED BY RUDOLF VON LABAN, 1934
This image captures the opening night of Laban's 1934 production at the Allied State Theatre in Berlin. Laban was already developing his movement theory.

Pick and mix what you like

Clearly, all this detailed work is a rehearsal and developmental tool to help you make choices about how you use your body. When you are performing, you should be totally involved in pursuing your character's wants. Don't get too bogged down with the technicalities of Laban if it doesn't help you, but don't shy away from challenging yourself physically. Take what you can use and add it to your toolbox.

LABAN QUESTIONS

You can also analyse the movement by asking questions such as:

- Which parts of my body do I move?
- Where does the movement start?
- How does it spread through my body?
- How large is my kinesphere?
- Where is the movement going?

'THE TYGER', LABAN-STYLE

Choose a stanza from the poem 'The Tyger' by William Blake and perform it using Laban's Effort Actions. Begin by studying the text and write down effort actions, such as 'flick' or 'float', next to certain phrases, words or even syllables, and especially the verbs. Explore the transitions between the different Effort Actions. Then perform the stanza using words and movement. Notice how the movements complement or contrast with the thoughts, how much colour and subtlety is available to you. Take the movements to their extremes, then bring them down so that they are barely perceptible, while maintaining the effort action. Repeat four times, paying special attention to each of the four Motion Factors: Space, Time, Weight and Flow.

> To mime is to literally embody and therefore understand better. A person who handles bricks all day long reaches a point where he no longer knows what he is handling. It has become an automatic part of his physical life. If he is asked to mime the object, he rediscovers the meaning of the object, its weight and volume. This has interesting consequences for our teaching method: miming is a way of rediscovering a thing with renewed freshness.
>
> Jacques Lecoq

JACQUES LECOQ

Jacques Lecoq (1921–1999), a French actor, mime, and acting instructor, founded L'École Internationale de Théâtre in Paris in 1956. Many top actors have trained there, including Geoffrey Rush (*Shine*) and Toby Jones (*Infamous*), as well as Simon McBurney and Annabel Arden, founding members of world-renowned physical-based theater company Complicité.

THE LECOQ-TRAINED ACTOR

GEOFFREY
RUSH IN *SHINE*,
DIRECTED
BY SCOTT
HICKS, 1966
Rush trained
at L'École
Internationale
de Théâtre with
Jacques Lecoq
in 1975.

Physical poetry

Lecoq came to theatre from a background in gymnastics, and as a teacher of physical education for several years. He came to understand movement as a kind of physical poetry, and as a trainer of actors he aimed to nurture the unique creativity of the individual performer, rather than take a one-size-fits-all approach. One of the key exercises in Lecoq training is Neutral Mask, which makes the actor aware of their individual habits and tendencies, so they can move beyond them to become someone else.

CHARACTER TECHNIQUE

TOBY JONES WITH DIRECTOR DOUGLAS
MCGRATH, ON SET SHOOTING *INFAMOUS*, 20
Toby Jones garnered critical praise for his
nuanced and flamboyant performance as Capote

TOBY JONES'S CAPOTE

Toby Jones describes how he approached the challenging role of Truman Capote
in the movie *Infamous*: 'I'm always interested in knowing what a character looks
like when he's in a neutral state. Not angry or sad, but just walking down a
corridor … If I'm playing a real character, I'll watch endless footage and try
to reach an understanding of what that person looked like — and behaved like —
in a neutral state of being.' For Capote's voice, he looked at the anatomy of
the man's jaw and the size of his tongue (very long). He discovered that he
had been ashamed of his teeth, and he probably spoke loudly because he had
grown up with four old women. His research gave him a 'set of physical
mnemonics — he breathes like this, his gait is like this — that help[ed] me to
check in and out of a character.'

Key principles

The three skills that Lecoq fosters are *le jeu* (playfulness), *complicité* (togetherness) and *disponsibilité* (openness), and quite a lot of time is spent learning to become a clown. While Method-based acting focuses on drawing on your own sense memories and experience, Lecoq's approach looks outwards. It is a training in observation – observing the world anew. You learn about character through observing behaviour as well as objects.

NEUTRAL STATE

The Lecoq approach to character is to find their neutral state. Instead of looking at the words in a script and trying to work out the character from the words, you start from the neutral physicality and a point of silence, then try to find how the words came about, the impulse that caused those words to come out of the silence.

Lecoq encouraged his actors to explore ways of expression that fitted their individuality. Exploratory mime was one of his means of doing this.

FELDENKRAIS METHOD

Israeli physicist Dr Moshé Feldenkrais (1904–84) started to develop a dynamic method during the 1940s in response to his own crippling knee injury. He risked becoming a paraplegic if he underwent surgery, so began his quest to heal himself and improve human functioning by increasing self-awareness through a programme of gentle, focused movement.

Body teaches brain

Feldenkrais believed that the mind and the body are one and he devised a series of quiet, exploratory exercises that allow the brain to learn new skills, to evoke new neuromuscular patterns of organic movement and thought. The exercises are slow, gentle and controlled. They are process-oriented rather than goal-oriented, and the importance lies in the attention that is given to the movement. Feldenkrais deepens the awareness of how you use your body, and teaches you strategies to minimise effort and increase the quality of the movement. This leads to better coordination, posture, flexibility, balance, precision and spontaneity. An essential part of the method is that the body can actually teach the brain.

Practitioners use their hands to guide the movement of a client, who may be sitting, lying or standing. This 'hands-on' technique helps the student experience connections between various parts of the body.

AWARENESS-RAISING

The exercises break down movement into their smallest components and look at them in relation to gravity, so that you learn the most effective way of moving. It not only enhances fitness and performance, but it also helps you to subtly change your thought processes so you can handle situations in daily life more easily, and gives you a better sense of awareness generally. A key Feldenkrais question is 'What will best serve my intentions?' This is especially useful for the actor, who must be focused on the intentions of the character they are playing. Also, truthful acting is efficient and doesn't waste energy. Do only what is required — any more is too much.

WHERE NEXT?

For more information read Feldenkrais's book *Awareness through Movement: Easy-to-Do Health Exercises to Improve Your Posture, Vision, Imagination, and Personal Awareness.* Alternatively, take classes with a teacher who is a Guild-Certified Feldenkrais Practitioner (GCFP).

PETER BROOK

Feldenkrais worked with Peter Brook in Paris for several years. Brook said of Feldenkrais: 'He has studied the body in movement with a precision that I found nowhere else.'

ANIMAL WORK

Animal work has three main benefits for the actor. First, it is an immediate and imaginative way to explore and develop a character both physically and psychologically (witness Marlon Brando's 'bulldog' Don Corleone in *The Godfather*, or Anthony Hopkins' reptilian Hannibal Lecter in *The Silence of the Lambs*). Second, it allows you to experience moment-to-moment action and reaction. Animals are driven by their wants, just like humans. However, as an animal, actors can really experience authentic pursuit of a want directly with all their physical being, instinctively, and without intellectualising and without a script. Third, you can experience the physical and psychological action working together organically, which is what you must do when performing. When you are being an animal, you stop intellectualising, which permits an instinctive response to your needs and your environment.

'THE BULLDOG'

MARLON BRANDO STARS IN *THE GODFATHER*, DIRECTED BY FRANCIS FORD COPPOLA, 1972
Marlon Brando used an animal image of a bulldog shot in the neck. This unique physicality and the intelligence and humanity of his characterisation earned him his second Oscar.

Observation

Go to the zoo and observe several animals. Watch videos as well, so you can see them in their natural habitat. Choose some that fascinate you and others with which you find it harder to identify. Observe their movements and how they interact with their environment. Think about what drives each animal; what it wants. Imagine yourself in its position and try to see the world through its eyes. Research its environment, and read up about whatever aspects interest you about its character or physiology.

ESSENCE OF ANIMAL

It is important to remember that, when you come to 'be' an animal, it is not an intellectual exercise. No planning, no preconceptions. Forget about everything you have read and don't approach the exercise with a bunch of ideas to try out. Trust that what you have observed and learned is in your memory and subconscious, so when you become the animal you will find its essence — you won't be thinking about your research or trying to force the exercise in a particular direction. Don't worry about how your body shape differs from that of the animal, because you will be exploring the essence, experiencing its inner life and rhythms rather than simply representing its physical form. Let your physicality develop naturally and be led by the essence of the animal.

Observing birds can give you a great appreciation of grace, formation and the pace of movement.

Unexpected external stimuli from another actor gives you the opportunity to respond instinctively in-the-moment.

ANIMAL OBSERVATION

Base your animal work on research and observation, otherwise you will rely on clichés and generalisations.

BECOME THE ANIMAL

Allow your identification with the animal to emerge slowly, and don't move unless it comes from your new animal being. Gradually you will start thinking like the animal — you will start to feel its drives and it will move you into action. Don't move until the animal's essence and wants drive you to move. Allow these drives to consume you. The partner will put obstacles in your way, and make unexpected noises. You will respond instinctively with movement, vocalisations, and you will find you are affected emotionally, unplanned, uninhibited. Accept your new animal structure, both its limitations and its new-found freedoms, without judgement.

Transformation

Animal work is best done in a group, or with another person, because you need them to supply unexpected external stimuli. Lie on your back on the floor and spend at least 10 minutes clearing your mind, focusing on your breathing. Quieten the human you in preparation for receiving the animal. See how close you can get to falling asleep without dropping off. Now gradually bring your consciousness towards the animal and allow the animal to come into you. Don't force anything. The simple act of mentally starting the process will be enough for the change to start affecting your subconscious.

Moving on

It is impossible in this short section to present a thorough overview of animal work. For a more detailed explanation, see Moni Yakim's wonderful book *Creating a Character: A Physical Approach to Acting*.

ANALYSIS

After the exploration phase (at least half an hour), spend 10 minutes writing a short paragraph (150 words maximum) about your experience. Underline important phrases, especially the verbs, adjectives and adverbs, as these will show you clearly the wants of the animal and will give you character choices. For example, if you were an octopus, you might write 'I wanted to attach myself to everything.' This could be a big discovery for playing a character for whom that single character choice applies.

JERZY GROTOWSKI – LES EXERCISES PLASTIQUES

Polish theatre director Jerzy Grotowski (1933–99) was one of the twentieth century's greatest innovators. He is famous for his notion of 'Poor Theatre', that of taking away everything that distracts the audience from the actor and stripping the actor to reveal their real incarnate self.

Jerzy Grotowski, stage director and pioneer of experimental theatre in Poland, standing outside the Polski Theatre in Wroclaw, c.1966.

Grotowski devised a series of physical isolations, which he called 'Les Exercises Plastiques'. They are very challenging, but the physical difficulty is a valuable part of the emotional experience — feelings of frustration, anger, fear and insecurity are accessed purely through attempting these difficult exercises. The perfection of the techniques is not as important as the awareness of the process, however.

Alternate realities

Grotowski held that 'memories are always physical reactions. It is our skin which has not forgotten, our eyes which have not forgotten.' He believed that we can release the emotions and the imaginative truth through the physical body. The instinct to contact and accept alternate realities – to make believe – is easily accessible to us in childhood, but we lose it as we grow older and are forced to restrain our emotions and natural impulses. Grotowski shows that if we activate our bodies, we unlock the emotional freedom we experienced as children. This is a quasi-spiritual quest, which demands complete dedication and sacrifice from the actor. For this reason, many have rejected his work as too angst-ridden and demanding.

The Teatr Polski Bydgoszcz, in Wroclaw, Poland. It still has a cutting-edge programme of theatre and festivals today.

Removing the masks

Just as Poor Theatre stripped away all the lighting, props and staging that detracted from the actor, so Grotowski aimed to strip away the blocks of the actor to achieve 'integration, the discarding of masks, the revealing of the real substance: a totality of physical and mental reactions'. The actor's first duty, he said, 'is to grasp the fact that nobody here wants to give him anything; instead they plan to take a lot from him, to take away that to which he is usually very attached: his resistance, reticence, his inclination to hide behind masks, his half-heartedness, the obstacles his body places in the way of his creative act, his habits, and even his usual "good manners"'.

By stripping away theatrical devices such as stage design, lighting and costume, Grotowski allowed the skills of the actor to become the primary spectacle.

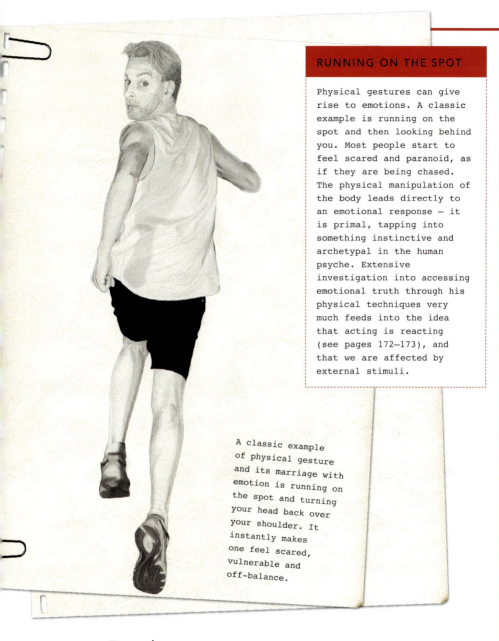

Physical gestures can give rise to emotions. A classic example is running on the spot and then looking behind you. Most people start to feel scared and paranoid, as if they are being chased. The physical manipulation of the body leads directly to an emotional response — it is primal, tapping into something instinctive and archetypal in the human psyche. Extensive investigation into accessing emotional truth through his physical techniques very much feeds into the idea that acting is reacting (see pages 172–173), and that we are affected by external stimuli.

A classic example of physical gesture and its marriage with emotion is running on the spot and turning your head back over your shoulder. It instantly makes one feel scared, vulnerable and off-balance.

Read on…

For a detailed examination of how Jerzy Grotowski's physical exercises can open a pathway to the actor's inner creativity, read *An Acrobat of the Heart* by teacher-director-playwright Stephen Wangh.

7
SCREEN ACTING

Screen acting isn't simply about doing less, nor is it intrinsically more 'truthful' than stage acting. The camera exposes artifice, for sure, but in this highly technical medium, shooting out of sequence, hitting your mark, cheating shots or talking to thin air and imagining things that aren't there, makes finding your reality even more demanding than in the theatre. Shooting is more about results than process, hence the old adage that plays are performed while movies are made. Your character is still driven by the same objectives, but the way you express them is different. This chapter introduces some of the challenges facing the modern screen actor.

> # If theatre acting is an operation with a scalpel, movie acting is an operation with a laser.
>
> Michael Caine

THE DIFFERENCES BETWEEN STAGE AND SCREEN

The technical requirements of stage and screen present different challenges, but your psychological preparation as an actor in the role should be identical. Quite simply, in both you need to know where you are in the story so you can pursue your character's objectives moment by moment, without banging into the furniture or fluffing your lines. That's all. The essential difference is that on screen it's more of a juggling act – you've got a little technical monitor going on subconsciously, about the framing of the shot, making sure you hit your mark and that your continuity works.

Being truthful

Actors too often get sidetracked by the idea that stage and screen demand different truthfulness, realism and scale, but to focus on being 'truthful' is a big mistake. You can't 'be' truthful, just as you can't 'be' intense or magnetic. Focus on the process and on the technical requirements, and those things will come. Besides, filming often requires you to cheat things that wouldn't happen in real life, but they work on screen and give the required effect to the audience.

Acting for screen can be a juggling act – there can be many more things to take into consideration than on stage.

Authenticity

Film acting doesn't always feel more 'real' to the actor than theatre; it feels more authentic to the audience. Remember that it's your job to take part in this highly technical process to make that happen, so it's often more about creating that illusion than having an acting epiphany.

Study the restaurant scene in *Heat* — one of the most intense movie scenes of all time. Robert De Niro and Al Pacino are driving actions against huge obstacles. They aren't indulging emotions, or trying to be intense or truthful. However, the more you watch the scene, the more you will realise how technical the whole process is. Be sure that every single eye movement, every pause, every thought, is executed with the precision of masters of their craft who are in complete control of every nanosecond of what they are doing in front of the camera. Trust that the psychological process and the attention to detail are the same, but that the technical demands are different. If you want to be truthful and intense on screen, think more thoughts — because less is *not* more.

INTENSITY ON SCREEN

ROBERT DE NIRO AND AL PACINO IN *HEAT*, DIRECTED BY MICHAEL MANN, 1995

Every eye movement and facial gesture in this famous restaurant scene is the result of brave acting choices and flawless screen technique.

> # The camera lies all the time; lies 24 times a second.
>
> Brian De Palma

Tell the story

Films are rarely shot in sequence, so it can be harder for an actor to know where they are in their character arc. But you must, so do whatever helps you achieve this. Write down and plan the journey of your character, scene to scene. Some actors use index cards for this: one for each scene, what happens before and after, and other conditioning factors such as the weather, cold or hunger. Include your objective for the start of the scene and any changes during the scene. You can also add any other information that links in with other scenes.

ENERGY LEVELS

A day in the theatre is very structured and reasonably predictable so you can pace yourself accordingly. Films are more unpredictable and more about conserving energy. You've got to stay calm and relaxed while you are waiting for hour on hour between takes, and then be fully switched on when it's your turn. You can't spend 16 hours in a state of frenzied expectation, so you have to learn when to switch on and off and practise calm readiness, especially if you've got a small part in a big film. Stay calm, do what is required of you and be professional.

THE SCRIPT

The script is ever evolving
during filming, which usually
only happens in the theatre
with new plays. Therefore you
need to be able to assimilate
new material at short notice.

The set

On stage, you may start blocking in the first week of rehearsals; on screen, the first time you see
the set is before your first take. On stage, you have complete freedom to move anywhere your
impulses tell you. On screen, you have to know the size of the shot and hit your marks. The
camera sees in depth, whereas on stage we think in terms of breadth. There is little time for
experimenting in films. You should arrive on set with a lot of choices already made, such
as blocking and business.

There is
little time to
adjust to your
environment on
set, so you
must already
have made
strong choices
beforehand.

LEARNING YOUR LINES

A few theatre actors like to turn up to the first day of stage rehearsals with their lines learnt, but when you arrive for a film shoot you must know all your lines inside out — and have made choices about how you will play them, and then be prepared to play them in different ways. Also, you may turn up on set to be told you're filming a scene that was originally scheduled weeks away. The good news is that you'll only be shooting a few minutes of screen time each day for films (more for TV).

You must know your lines and feel completely confident with them before you start a screen project, due to time constraints.

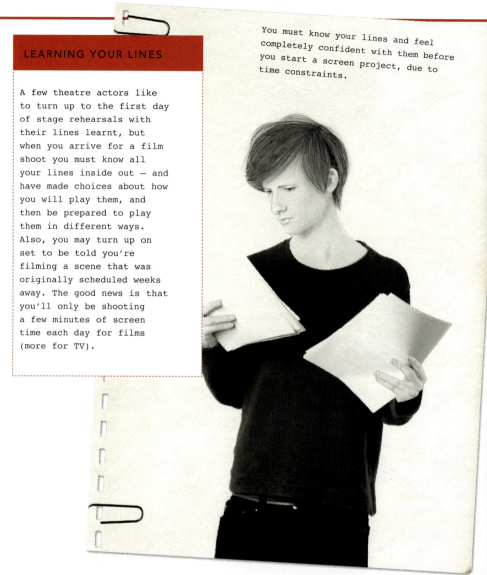

Automatic pilot

You must be prepared to take direction and shoot the scene however the director wants it. There are so many other factors that will demand your concentration during the shoot – hitting your mark, maintaining continuity, ignoring the camera and crew, coping with an unfamiliar set, performing with actors you've only just met – that, unless your lines are completely automatic, you will be overwhelmed.

KEEPING OCCUPIED ON SET

GINA LOLLOBRIGIDA BEHIND
THE SCENES WHILE FILMING
COME SEPTEMBER, DIRECTED BY
ROBERT MULLIGAN, 1961.

WORD PERFECT

Learn the thoughts behind the
lines that lead to the
words. Practise saying them
in lots of different ways —
don't get fixed into a line
reading. You have to reach
the point where you own the
words, and don't have to
think about them, so during
the take you can concentrate
on your objective, as
well as all the other
unfamiliar business.

Rehearsals

In the theatre if you're lucky you'll have a minimum of four weeks' rehearsal, but in films there's a sliding scale from some to none, so you've got to do lots more preparation at home, and then be flexible on set. The takes are like rehearsals, except that each requires performance quality and commitment. You must also keep emotional and physical continuity between takes, rather than try out lots of wild new things. Finally, you don't get any say about which take ends up in the final cut.

Imagination

The technicalities of film making often mean that you have to draw more on your imagination than you do on the stage, where you have the continuity of the play to help your reality. You may have to play an intense scene, while a stand-in supplies the other actor's lines off camera. If the scene involves a lot of CGI, you may have to stare at a cross drawn somewhere, or a stick that is supposed to represent a person.

PLAYING TO THE CAMERA

Adding a frame alters the audience's perception of reality, and directs their attention to what the director wants them to see. Screen acting is highly technical, so you need to be aware of camera position and what type of shot it is taking – then forget about it. The idea of 'playing to the camera' is as unhelpful to your truthfulness as an actor as 'playing to the audience'. Your main focus should be on what your character wants in a given moment and listening to the other actors.

EXTREME CLOSE UP

GRACE KELLY AND JAMES STEWART IN *REAR WINDOW*, 1954, DIRECTED BY ALFRED HITCHCOCK This classic uses extreme close ups, particularly of Grace Kelly's face. This technique is used to create claustrophobic tension and develop the theme of obsessed voyeurism.

LET THE CAMERA FIND YOU

The underlying principles of acting are the same, regardless of the medium, so be aware of the size of shot, but focus on your reality within the scene. Don't think of projecting or telegraphing anything to the camera — ignore it and trust that it will 'find' you. Furthermore, human beings hide their thoughts and emotions all the time, so truthful acting is often more about what your character tries to hide than what you, the actor, can reveal. This is why, for example, someone trying not to cry is often more moving than them all-out blubbing.

'THE CAMERA CAN PHOTOGRAPH THOUGHT.'

DIRK BOGARDE

The basic camera shots

Adjust your performance accordingly. Ask the camera operator if you are unsure what shot will happen during the take. Project your voice as far as the other actors (not as far as the camera).

01 EXTREME LONG SHOT

The camera is far away filming a panoramic view of an exterior location, so you will be a speck in the distance.

02 LONG SHOT

If you were performing on stage the camera is at the back of the theatre.

03 FULL SHOT

Shows the whole body.

04 MEDIUM SHOT

Knees to waist up.

05 MEDIUM CLOSE UP

Concentrates on a relatively small object such as your face.

06 EXTREME CLOSE UP

Shows a part of the face such as eyes or mouth.

Smaller shot, more precise

Adjust your performance accordingly. Become more concentrated as the size of shot decreases. This is the opposite of giving a smaller performance, or trying to be stiller. In close up you have to increase the intensity, and think more precisely and attentively, rather than make your face immobile. Project your voice as far as the other actors/the microphone (but not as far as the camera). If you are unsure about the size of shot, ask the camera operator, and, if you want to be really diplomatic, ask for the cut-off point. Don't ask the director – they may think you are only concerned with close ups, and may not appreciate that you need to be able to fit some business into the frame or adjust your performance.

GOLDEN RULES

- Don't stop acting until the assistant director or the director says, 'Cut!' — even if you get something wrong.
- Do remember what you did in each take, so that you can repeat it exactly when you shoot different angles and reverses.
- Do come with all your lines learnt and business planned.
- Do add extra ideas and make suggestions, so long as you understand what is technically possible.

HITTING YOUR MARK

Hitting your mark is one of the most important requirements of a screen actor. You can give the best performance of your life, but if you are in the wrong place when you do it, you'll be wrongly lit, out of focus and even out of frame, so always make sure that you're always in the right place at the right time.

'X' marks the spot

A mark is a piece of tape or a chalk mark (usually an 'X' or 'T', or even a twig or stone if you are outside) that indicates where the actor should stand, or where he or she should come to a stop. The best way to hit your mark when walking is to stand on your mark and then walk backwards saying your dialogue; the spot where you reach the end of your speech is where you start. When you have to move between two fixed marks, then you have to practise saying the lines while walking, so that you can learn the pace of your walking and the speech.

ON YOUR MARKS

The marks get set during rehearsals, so the best way to hit them without looking down is to find visual markers at eye level, such as furniture, or to line up two objects. If you are outside, use trees and other features. Don't use the positions of other actors for your blocking, as they may be inconsistent or wrong.

It's tough when take one is technically okay and take two has better acting. Out here [Hollywood] they print the first one. That's the one where we all hit the mark on the floor and who cares about the acting.

Judy Holliday

USING YOUR EYES

When you look at something, one of your eyes will be dominant. If you are being shot in close up, don't change the focus from one eye to the other. For continuity's sake, always lead with the same eye for the same shot. When you are looking at another actor, look at one of their eyes; don't dart your focus around the face, nose and eyes, as you would in real life. It can feel artificial, but unless you keep your eye movements specific and minimal your eyes will look ridiculous on screen.

Keep an eye on your eyes

Maintaining eye contact with another actor may give you the illusion that you are sharing, or that you are really connecting with them as an actor, but we don't stare people out in real life, unless in a face-to-face confrontation. Excessive eye contact is particularly unhelpful on screen, because often the camera needs to be able to see your thoughts – which it can't do when your eyes are glaring at someone else. If you use excessive eye contact in acting, there's a good chance you are telegraphing, either to the audience or to the other actor. In fact, our eyes rarely make contact with other people's. This is even more true on film, where for the sake of the shot you may be talking to the back of the other person's head, so the camera can see both of you.

WATCH YOUR FACE

Be aware of every eye movement, because when you get in front of a camera in close-up, every facial movement becomes a character choice. For example, if you blink frequently, it makes your character appear weak; if you make a conscious effort not to blink, your character will appear strong, both as a character and in terms of your screen presence. That doesn't mean you should never blink on screen, but this example gives you an illustration of how aware you must be of your movements.

X-ray vision

If you need to make eye contact, but you can't see the other person's eyes (maybe you are standing behind them), then look through the obstacle to where their eyes would be. This will read as eye contact on screen, without you having to crane your head round unnaturally.

CLOSE-UP SHOTS

RICHARD ATTENBOROUGH IN *THE LAST GRENADE*, DIRECTED BY GORDON FLEMYNG, 1970

Attenborough during takes. Behind his back, appropriately for the plot, are Stanley Baker (Major Grigsby) and Honor Blackman, who plays the general's wife having an affair with the major.

USING YOUR VOICE

Speaking on camera demands the same technique as on the stage – breath rooted and supported in the diaphragm (see pages 102–105). You can't use your ordinary naturalistic speaking voice because, unless the breath is rooted, it will lack depth, tone and subtlety, and it won't be fully available to express your thoughts and connect to your emotions.

THE MICROPHONE

As a general rule you project to the other person as far as the microphone is from you. For example, if you were in close up speaking to someone standing 5 metres away, you should talk very quietly, even though in real life the other person wouldn't be able to hear you. That's why the microphone position is a good guide.

SECOND NATURE

Ideally, you should become so accustomed to supporting your breath that you will do it all the time, even when you aren't on stage or being filmed. If this feels artificial, it means you haven't consolidated the technique – and it probably sounds artificial, too. If you practise supporting the breath in your everyday life, eventually it will become second nature.

It is important to be aware of where the boom microphone is in relation to the shot.

Vocal levels

When we talk in real life, the volume depends on our emotional state and how far away the listener is. In the theatre, there is the added consideration of the farthest member of the audience. However, in movies you only project as far as the person to whom you are speaking (and often a lot less) – but this is determined by the *size of the shot*, not the actual distance between. In a long shot it's about 3 metres; in a medium close-up it's approximately 1 metre; and it's about 15 cm away in close up.

Keep a number of factors in mind – for instance, how close the camera is to you, as well as how far the person you are talking to may be from you.

Pacing and volume traps

When acting for the screen, however, there are some pacing and volume traps to avoid.

1 If you are in close up, resist the temptation to slow down and reduce your energy level. You must keep the same level of intensity and pace, but reduce the volume. This feels artificial, but it works on camera.

2 In wide shots, sometimes the boom can't get close enough to you without appearing in frame, or casting shadows, so you may be asked to speak more loudly. When you need to produce extra volume, don't push – now, more than ever, you need to remain centred.

3 Sometimes the sound technician will ask you for more volume, but you might feel it is wrong for the size of shot. If in doubt, ask the director, because you don't want to come across as over-acting just to make the sound technician's job easier. Besides, the scene will be shot from many different angles and sizes, so frequently the director will match the shot to the vocal level during editing.

4 When filming in front of a studio audience, don't project to them!

STAGE VERSUS SCREEN

Don't equate increased volume with increased emotional intensity, on stage and screen — the opposite is often more interesting, and compulsory if you are in close up. On stage the actor is responsible for pacing the speech, but on film the pace is created in the editing suite. This means you can be more flexible and allow the words to flow more naturalistically, as your thoughts create them.

The filming process involves long working days (and nights) so it is important that you protect your voice by drinking plenty of water and saving your energy — even when people are rushing around you!

PHYSICAL AND EMOTIONAL CONTINUITY

Physical continuity from take to take is important. If you hold a spoon in your right hand during a take, then it's your job to remember which hand you used, or which word of dialogue you were saying when you picked it up, or turned your head or put it to your mouth.

Attention to detail

Emotional continuity involves knowing where you are in your character arc, but also maintaining the same emotional intensity and pitch between the master shot and other takes. If spontaneity is your driving force, and you can't be bothered with such technicalities, you won't get very far as a screen actor. These technical requirements *are* film acting. Good acting in any medium is about preparation and planning – spontaneity comes way down the list, and is only achieved and earned by your meticulous attention to detail.

Don't trick the editor

Some actors play continuity tricks to make sure that the editor can't cut away. A classic ruse is to take off your glasses at the beginning of a speech and put them on at the end. Keep business simple and repeatable and try to make everyone look good.

PLAN YOUR MOVEMENTS

The continuity person is there to makes notes of every movement and costume details, but it's your responsibility to get it right, because if you can't remember what you did in the master shot, and then start doing something else altogether in the succeeding shots, you'll make life impossible for everyone, and you'll be wasting time and money. You should come to the shoot with all your business and movement mapped out, avoiding complicated, fiddly business that you can't replicate. Otherwise, some of your best work will be unusable because of continuity issues.

THE CONTINUITY EDITOR

A camera crew on location making a television programme. The woman in the foreground is a continuity editor working on set — she is timing all the takes and making notes to help editing during post-production. It is difficult for inconsistencies to get past someone like this on set, but continuity is still primarily the actor's responsibility.
Be consistent in your movements in each take, otherwise your best work may be unusable. The other end of the spectrum is that it causes a blunder in the final cut. We have all seen or heard about a film with a continuity 'blooper'.

REACTION SHOTS

Reaction shots are taken in close up and show an actor without dialogue reacting to what another actor is saying, or what is happening in the scene. This is where your listening skills really come to the fore. All you can do is listen to what they are saying and allow yourself to react honestly. However, you are still pursuing your character's objective, and if you really listen to what they are saying, your thoughts and responses will be truthful because they will be connected to your wants, or your obstacles.

CONTINUOU
REACTIONS

PENELOPE CRUZ IN *VOLVER*, DIRECTED BY PEDRO ALMODÓVAR, 2006.

WHO'S THERE?

The other actor may be generous and feed you lines off camera with the same intensity as if they were being filmed, and contort themselves so they can get into your eye line beside the camera. However, many actors prefer to do their reaction shots without anyone else reading in, and you may also find that the other actor isn't available — then, you'll get a member of the crew reading in a flat voice and giving you very little. Here's another instance where your inner life has to be rock solid and your imagination comes to your rescue.

Pursue the want

Many actors will tell you just to listen, but this isn't enough. You must also be playing your character's want; otherwise, your reaction will have no context and you won't 'know' how to react. You always pursue the want, even when you are listening, because it determines how you listen and how the other person's words and actions affect you.

Pulling faces?

Although it goes against all Method training, sometimes you will be requested to over-act. You mustn't forget that there will be plenty of times when the director will ask for reactions from you that feel little more than pulling faces for the close up. Go with it, though, and you'll be pleased by the results on camera, even if you felt less 'real' while doing it.

TRUTHFULNESS

On other occasions, the director will ask you to do a movement or look in a certain direction, and when it appears on screen, what the audience reads into your action may be very different from what you were really feeling or thinking. In the end, what is truthful and effective for the audience isn't always what makes the actor feel most truthful or comfortable. This contradiction lies at the heart of film acting, which is why it is wrong to say that acting in films is more 'real' – often, for the actor it can feel technical and untruthful. So long as the director keeps quiet, you're doing a good job.

Reaction shots may be filmed out of context, hours or days after they feature in the scene in question.

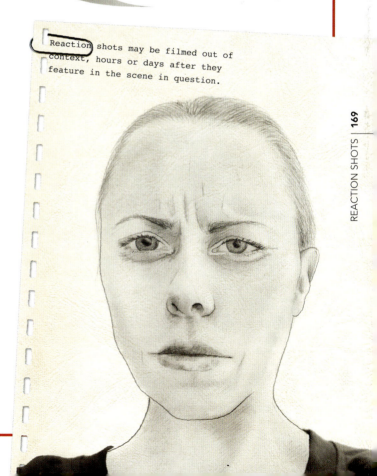

8

ACTING IN THE MOMENT

Certain phrases are ever present in acting circles, such as 'acting is reacting', 'less is more' and 'take risks', and actors are forever stressing the importance of 'listening'. But none of this advice really connects until you gain experience, and it can even be damaging outside its proper context. Ultimately all acting technique is only useful if it works for you, so it is crucial that you address your strengths and weaknesses and take responsibility for developing your own process. We all work in different ways, so this chapter offers some universal gleanings to loosen you up and complement formal technique.

ACTING IS REACTING

How you pursue your wants as a character is directed towards how you want to make the other character feel. The audience are interested in this, too, which is why, in films, they will often watch the listener rather than the speaker, because they want to see how that person is feeling, how they are reacting. Acting as reacting is important to remember in all forms of acting, but it is often most noticeable in films for good reasons.

IN-THE-MOMENT RESPONSES

By reacting, you truly pursue your want in the moment to what the other person has just done or said — not how they did it yesterday or in the last take. You respond to how they do it now, and the result is in-the-moment immediacy and truth. In life we are always looking for feedback (reactions), because we want to see how we are engaging others, how we are making them feel, and we, in turn, change our behaviour according to how they make us feel.

Theatre is a true actor's medium because the audience chooses where it places its attention, not the editor.

The golden rule in films is that you react before you speak. In real life, and often on the stage, our faces express what we have just said. The reverse is true in films: by the time you have finished speaking, the camera has already switched to the other person (if it was on you at all in the first place). Often the camera will cut away from you just before you finish speaking, so it can see how the other actor feels. Therefore, what you do after you have finished speaking usually doesn't appear, because to show it would slow down the pace.

No nesting in the theatre!

In a film, if you want to show something visually to the audience, do it before your line or in the middle of your speech, rather than at the end. In theatre this is called 'nesting' on your line and is discouraged. Not so in films – which is why you have to film so many reaction shots.

His face is looking forward, yet we are drawn to her reaction to move the story forward.

React to their acting

Another way acting is reacting is to do with listening. You react to what the other person does and says, because of how they make you feel; you also react to the obstacles, the surroundings and other conditioning factors, because they inform how you pursue your want.

> Emotion – it's like a fever chart – it takes us, we can't take it. Almost no emotion goes steadily upwards and then explodes – that's only a dramatic cliché. It goes up and down. In the middle of the deepest emotion sometimes you can be almost in shock so that you feel nothing.
>
> Uta Hagen

WANTING NOT FEELING

Emotion is a by-product

This quote from one of Uta Hagen's televised masterclasses wonderfully indicates how misguided it is for an actor to chase emotion, to seek it, to try to feel it. If you seek emotion you will fall unfailingly into cliché and fakery. You will indulge it, reveal too much to the audience and to the other characters and you will become gratingly unwatchable – actually succeeding in making the audience recoil and feel tense for all the wrong reasons. They may even feel embarrassed for you, or anger at being cheated of watching a real human being. What a shame: you're trying so hard, and now everyone hates you!

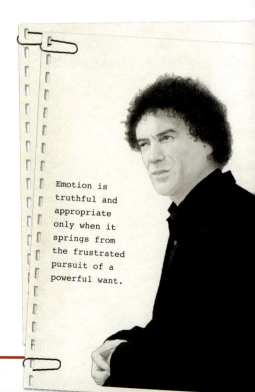

Emotion is truthful and appropriate only when it springs from the frustrated pursuit of a powerful want.

EXPECTATIONS

In acting as in life, we pursue our wants and we have expectations that are usually unmet, so we alter our behaviour moment to moment accordingly. We rarely get what we expect, and the dramatic tension and emotion often come when expectations are confounded. So, when you are acting, have big wants — but also think how the next moment will turn out. Acting is allowing oneself to be taken by surprise over and over again, just like in real life, where we can't predict the future.

Follow your want – feelings will follow

Don't plan where you're going to get emotional, or where you're going to do a certain gesture, or make a move. Only follow your want, and leave yourself alone. So long as you have done your homework – such as emotional memory or personalisation – and grounded the scene in specifics to make it real for you, the feelings will come naturally without being forced.

ATTIC MISCELLANY.
Theatrical Portraiture Nº 5.

How to look amorously

This page from the *Attic Miscellany Theatrical Portraiture*, printed in 1790, instructs how an actor could 'look amorously'. Even today clichéd gestures are more commonplace than you might think.

> Acting is not about having a 'bag of tricks' but about learning to remove the protective blocks that inhibit our natural responses. And then combining that childlike instinct with an adult sensibility and focus. It is about trusting the simplicity of an inner truth.
>
> Mel Churcher

USE WHATEVER WORKS

Peeling the layers

How you choose to do this is up to you. Some actors work from the outside in; others, from the inside out; or a mixture of both. Some find their way into a character through the physicality or the clothes – a pair of shoes or the set of the jaw. Other actors find the physicality as a result of exploring the character. Do whatever works for you, because there is no one single method that suits everyone.

A pair of shoes can alter the physicality and help you to discover your character.

INDIVIDUAL METHOD

Stanislavski devised his Method as a reaction to the highly stylised and theatrical acting that was popular at the time — even he said, 'There is only one Method, which is that of an organic, creative nature.' Early in his career he focused on creating truthful emotions and then embodying them, but as an old man he came to recognise that physical action can also inspire the emotion. His Method evolved and so should yours.

EXTREME METHOD ACTING

DANIEL DAY-LEWIS IN *THERE WILL BE BLOOD*,
DIRECTED BY PAUL THOMAS ANDERSON, 2007
Reclusive and reluctant star Day-Lewis insists on
living each role for up to two years before shooting
a new movie.

Use your tools

Do not worship any method. Use
technique as tools to create reality
for you. The reality impacts. No one
admires the tools – who cares about
Michelangelo's chisels? Any Method
also depends very much upon
the style of play, or the medium –
theatre, TV or film.

'WHAT IS IMPORTANT IN ANY ACTING TECHNIQUE IS NOT THE ANSWERS IT PROVIDES BUT RATHER THE SPACE IT OFFERS FOR YOU TO PROPOUND THE MOST IMPORTANT QUESTIONS FOR YOURSELF. WHAT PARTICULAR CHALLENGES DO YOU ENCOUNTER IN YOUR ACTING?… WHAT MAKES ACTING TRULY ALIVE FOR YOU?'

STEPHEN WANGH

Acting comes easily to everybody. All I've done is simply, through the extraordinary talents of Stella Adler, who was my teacher and mentor, learned how to be aware of the process… in life… how to be aware of my feelings.

Marlon Brando

"

BEHAVING TRUTHFULLY

Observe yourself

Actors are often criticised for being self-centred, and rightly so, because a big ego and an exclusive focus on the self can stop you from closely observing the behaviour of others. However, every character you play comes from within you, so hours of self-observation are mandatory. If you want to recreate an emotional life, but especially a physical reality, in performance, then you need to be able to observe and remember how you behave in various conditions and circumstances in daily life. It is the single most important skill an actor can develop.

Observing yourself in the mirror as you think a monologue in your head, or speaking the text quietly, can help you explore an intimate naturalism.

REHEARSE AND BUILD

The more rehearsal and homework self-observation off stage you do, the more truthful and spontaneous you can be in your acting. Just because the truth is inside you doesn't mean that truthfulness is shrinking the reality, making it smaller. Reality can be huge if it is truthfully lived. Many film actors don't like to rehearse too much because they are afraid it will take away their spontaneity. Start with the sense of place, ground yourself in place and make it real and personal — every single detail — and you can build from there. Without place, you have nothing.

Use rehearsals to take risks and try new things without fear of failure.

Leave yourself free

As you rehearse, doing it and doing it and leaving it free, each time something new will happen. If something is correct, you'll probably stick to it, but if you keep something just for its effect, it will be dead. A performance grows with the detail – and it takes time. It can't all be there at once, unless it's a clichéd quick fix, so build, build, build. On stage or on screen, hear what you hear and see what you see, and go with it. Don't give yourself bad stage directions – there are plenty of bad directors around who will do that for you, so don't do it to yourself!

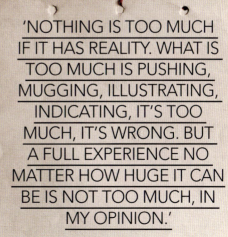

'NOTHING IS TOO MUCH IF IT HAS REALITY. WHAT IS TOO MUCH IS PUSHING, MUGGING, ILLUSTRATING, INDICATING, IT'S TOO MUCH, IT'S WRONG. BUT A FULL EXPERIENCE NO MATTER HOW HUGE IT CAN BE IS NOT TOO MUCH, IN MY OPINION.'

UTA HAGEN

> Suit the action to the word, the word to the action, with this special observance, that you o'erstep not the modesty of nature.
>
> Hamlet, Act III, Scene II

LESS IS MORE

Less is more?

Less is more is one of the most misunderstood ideas in acting. This mantra appears in many professional and artistic arenas, but it can be very unhelpful unless you are clear about what it really means. Unless you understand why you are being told to 'do less', it can become merely a sticking plaster that hides instead of fixes the problem. Instead of toning down an untruthful performance, address the root cause, which is always your attention to detail.

Specificity

Truth comes from *being specific*. When actors resort to generalisations, they mobilise all their acting fakery, often when they are under-prepared or the script is bad, to oversell themselves or the material. The end result is that maybe you over-project your voice, or are too emotional or use too much energy – all this has been caused because you are generalising. The director sees that you are doing too much and tells you to do less. What they should really say is 'be more specific'.

Not doing nothing

Less is more holds particular sway on film, but experienced film actors know, when the camera pulls in for a close-up shot, that they must do more, not less. They think more clearly, but they don't deliberately or consciously 'use their eyes and face more', rather they up the stakes of their wants and put tremendous concentration into their thoughts. Film actors often say that the audience does a lot of the work, which is true up to a point, but don't believe any actor who tells you that he is doing nothing!

MORE, MORE, MORE

Never do less. Always do more! More of the right things — focus on your wants, pursue them more completely, make your obstacles bigger, make your sense memories more detailed and specific, endow other actors and objects more completely, listen more openly.

BE TRUTHFUL

When a director tells you to 'do less', or 'less is more', what they really mean is that you are being untruthful. However, what you the actor take away from this is that somehow you must energise less, or move less, think less, feel less, show less, and before you know it you're completely blocked creatively.

SIMPLICITY IN PLOT; DEPTH IN ACTING

TIM ROBBINS AND MORGAN FREEMAN IN *THE SHAWSHANK REDEMPTION*, FRANK DARABONT, 1994

In this poignant and redemptive prison drama, the two lead actors give majestically understated performances as convicted murderers struggling to find meaning and purpose in their lives.

MAKING BRAVE CHOICES AND TAKING RISKS

Spend any time as an actor, and you'll hear everyone talking about this. Actors often attribute their own success to their ability to make brave choices and take risks, or cite it as their reason for admiring other actors. But what does it mean, and how do you know when you are doing it?

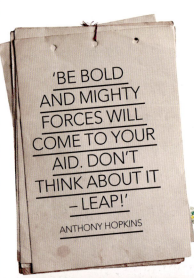

'BE BOLD AND MIGHTY FORCES WILL COME TO YOUR AID. DON'T THINK ABOUT IT – LEAP!'

ANTHONY HOPKINS

Supersize, then disguise

Playing a want like 'I want to destroy you' is much more powerful and easier than 'I want to make you feel uncomfortable.' Commit yourself physically to what your character wants and follow your impulses. If your character is hurting, make it shattering emotional pain, not just a minor irritation, and then decide how much of this pain you want to conceal from the other characters.

OUT ON A LIMB

First of all, you need to make your wants huge and the stakes high, both in your life and in your work. Your characters must have big and powerful drives — the extremes and possibilities are there for the taking. Accept the challenge and go out on a limb to find the character as they experience extreme moments in their lives, rather than shrinking everything down to your everyday humdrum level to make you more comfortable.

DARE TO FAIL

Have the courage to try things and get them wrong, because that's the only way you discover what you never imagined possible. Be prepared to fail and to expose yourself to criticism — expect it, because only by trying out extreme possibilities do you find what works for you. Also, the more you explore the boundaries, the more you push them back. Take everything to the limit and be flexible in your approach, rather than fall back on what you know worked last time.

RISK-TAKING PERFORMANCE

MERYL STREEP IN *SOPHIE'S CHOICE*, DIRECTED BY ALAN J. PAKULA,1982
Streep's vulnerability and high-stakes commitment to the role of Sophie is widely regarded as her finest screen achievement.

> The thing is doing it, that's what it's all about. Not in the results of it. After all what is a risk? It's a risk not to take risks. Otherwise, you can go stale and repeat yourself. I don't feel like a person who takes risks. Yet there's something within me that must provoke controversy because I find it wherever I go. Anybody who cares about what he does takes risks.
>
> Al Pacino

AVOIDING THE OBVIOUS

It is often said that if you tried to put real life on the stage, nobody would believe it. Extraordinary things happen in the real world that would seem implausible if put in front of an audience. However, when you use the magic 'what if', you can enjoy action on the stage or on film that no-one would believe in real life. Don't ask 'What would I do in this situation?' but instead 'What *could* my character do in this situation?' There's a whole universe of possibilities when you ask the right question.

MENACING PSYCHO OR OPENLY CULTURED?

Watch Anthony Hopkins make his first appearance on screen in *The Silence of the Lambs*. The audience has been primed to expect a slavering psychopath, but standing in his cell, hands lightly curled, he is an extraordinary assemblage of contradictions. He confounds expectations in so many ways. When he says, 'Good morning', he is gentle, cultured and open — the opposite of what the audience, and Jodie Foster's character, expects.

CONTRASTING PERFORMANCE

ANTHONY HOPKINS IN *THE SILENCE OF THE LAMBS*, DIRECTED BY JONATHAN DEMME, 1991.

Contrary Mary

Consider 'What if I were to do the exact opposite here?' Instead of shouting, how about speaking in a quiet voice? Instead of pausing, come in with your line right on top of your cue. Rather than showing your emotions, why not try to hide them? Look for the paradox between the inner character and the outer appearance – a loud and brash character may be concealing painful shyness, a villain can be charming and likable, a deeply selfish person may appear generous and an insecure person may feign confidence.

A good exercise in character is when you say the opposite of what you think the character would say or feel. It helps you to understand the subtext and your motivation.

BODY SAYS 'NO'

You avoid the obvious only by becoming obsessed with detail. The obvious is general, vague, surface, too naturalistic or too melodramatic, whereas the unexpected is subtle, detailed, expansive and deeply human. Human interaction is complex and multi-layered. We rarely say what we mean or mean what we say, and our body language often contradicts our words or our intentions. There is always a subtext, an agenda bubbling away beneath the surface. We appear to be doing one thing, but actually we're doing the opposite.

> What I do in the scene is not as important as what happens between me and the other person. And listening is what lets it happen. It's almost always the other person who causes you to say what you say next. You don't have to figure out how you'll say it. You have to listen so simply; so innocently, that the other person brings about a change in you that makes you say it and informs the way you say it.

LISTENING

Have you ever had a conversation with someone where you suddenly became self-conscious and couldn't concentrate on what they were saying because all you could think about was your separateness – you standing in your body, watching them standing in theirs? So you fix your stare and try really hard to look as though you are listening, but the more you do that, the more self-conscious you become. It's the same with acting. If you are too wrapped up in your own performance, you will stop listening, become self-conscious and give pre-planned responses.

Forget yourself

A lot of actors don't know how to listen – they know that listening is important, so they fix eye contact and really 'try' to listen. Real listening is about leaving yourself alone, forgetting about yourself and just allowing the other person to change you, to affect you emotionally.

ALAN ALDA (LEFT) STARS IN THE TV SERIES *M.A.S.H*, DIRECTED BY RICHARD ALTMAN, 1970.

OBEY YOUR IMPULSES

Listening to what the other person is saying gives you the impulse to speak (or keep quiet) — you aren't just waiting for them to finish saying their lines. Do not think about what you are going to say next or how you are going to say it. Listening takes you out of yourself and places all your focus on the other person. Imagine that: your body, your breathing, your whole being, focused on something other than itself. How liberating! If you let yourself be affected by what the other person is saying, then you don't have to worry about how to say your lines, or what to think — it will just happen.

Listen to their bodies

Listening doesn't just happen with your ears! While you are speaking, listen to what the other people are saying with their body language, their eyes, their physicality, their aura. When we speak we want to affect other people, so we focus even more on them than when we are silent. When you do this, you find that you are actually listening all the time.

Listening comes naturally to us in real life because we are motivated by our wants. When acting, treat listening as a way to further your character's wants.

9
SELLING YOURSELF

Acting is a business, and a successful career is built on business
and marketing skills, as well as acting talent and a bit of luck.
The more you understand how this side of the profession works,
the luckier you will get. It begins by identifying yourself as
a product and playing to your strengths with the perfect head
shot and CV, making an impression with casting directors and
auditioning effectively for stage and screen. All
of this supports you, the artist. The recognition and success that
comes from selling yourself properly leads to greater artistic
freedom and choice in the future.

LANDING AN AGENT

Getting an agent isn't essential, but without one you will miss out on a lot of casting opportunities that you either won't know about or won't be able to access. When casting directors need actors, they call agents – they don't call you. However, you still need to be proactive, so if you hear about a casting that you think would suit you, contact your agent and ask them to put you up for the part. An agent also increases your credibility because it demonstrates that someone else in the business believes you are commercial. Good agents are expert negotiators, who earn their 10–15 per cent (of your earnings) by getting you the best deal.

GREEDY OR HUNGRY?

The most important quality in an agent is that they are someone whom you trust and who is interested in developing your career rather than just making money. A big agency has lots of prestige and influence, but this doesn't guarantee your success, since the agents may be more focused on the millions they can make from their A-lister superstar clients than on you. Sometimes, therefore, a hungry and ambitious agent in a smaller, up-and-coming agency is preferable.

Making the first contact

Contact at least 20 agents – the more, the better. Send a head shot, CV and covering letter including details of your most impressive acting experience, and say that you are seeking representation. If you are appearing in a show, invite the agent to come and see you. Follow up with a phone call 10 days later and try to arrange a meeting. If you get no interest, contact another batch of agents, and consider changing your head shot.

The meeting

If an agent shows interest, the next step is meeting. Dress appropriately and, if you want to promote a certain character or look that demonstrates your casting type, do so, within reason. Bring your head shot, proof sheet showing all the photos taken during the shoot, your CV and showreel if you have one. Be prepared to perform a monologue or a sight-reading if required.

At the meeting, first impressions are key, so it is important to seem professional, prepared and aware of the kind of roles you will be good for.

How you dress can affect the kind of role that the agent thinks would work for you, so think carefully about this before you arrive.

Be proactive and realistic

Try to get feedback about your casting type, and what you can do to improve your castability. Find out who would be representing you within the agency and how many other clients they have in your category. Demonstrate that you have a realistic approach to the business of acting, and that you are proactive and ambitious (but without being arrogant or pushy). Ask how they would develop your career. If they spend the whole meeting talking about sending you up for corporate training films and you want prestigious theatre and film work, consider your options carefully.

KNOW YOUR TYPE

If the agent says he or she already has someone like you on the books, this may be true, or it may be a gentle letdown. Some people are lucky that they can easily be pigeonholed and get lots of agent interest, while others have to work hard to discover their casting niche — if you struggle to find work, and agents say you are 'difficult to cast' or 'will come into your own when you are older', you need to look again very closely at how you are presenting and marketing yourself in terms of your type (see pages 200—201).

Your agent should look over your CV and ask questions about points in your career so far. All the time they will be thinking about where you will fit in the industry.

Signing on with an agent

If an agent agrees to represent you, you will be given a contract to sign. Read it carefully; take it away and get legal advice if you feel out of your depth. Check out the commission rates, the conditions that allow both parties to terminate the arrangement and exclusivity details (eg, you may have a separate voiceover agent). Only sign on with an agent who is union-franchised (ie, regulated), and disregard any agent who asks for an upfront fee – reputable agents only take commission on your work.

This illustration from 1878 shows an actor with her agent — traditionally seen as untrustworthy and greedy individuals. Luckily this is an old-fashioned stereotype now as good agents will work hard in your best interest.

CV AND HEAD SHOTS

CV

Your CV should be a single sheet of paper, trimmed so that it fits exactly on the back of your photo (attach with staples). It should only show information that is relevant to your acting career (ie, no school, non-acting jobs or home address details).

What (not) to include

Include details of any drama training and classes. At the start of your career your CV should list all your acting experience, including parts played at college/drama school. As you gain more experience, you can delete the more trivial details as your prestigious work increases. Include the name of the production, your role, the director, studio name and television network. Don't list your commercials – instead put 'Commercial list available on request.' Otherwise, you could lose casting opportunities through a conflict of interest. It is also important not to lie about or exaggerate your appearance, skills or experience. Everyone has to start somewhere, so just be honest.

FACTS AND FIGURES

```
Use black ink on good-quality bond paper.
Keep the presentation simple and legible —
use just one font. At the top, put your
stage name, your contact number where you
can be reached at all times, agent name and
number and membership of any guilds or
unions. Underneath, add physical
characteristics such as eye and hair colour,
height and weight (playing age is optional,
but never put your actual age).
```

Only list skills you can do really well. For example, only include a foreign language if you speak it fluently; list regional or country accents, athletic skills, artistic skills and anything unusual that you can perform extremely well. Include driving licenses (full and clean).

Your CV needs to be as well-targeted as your presentation and attitude.

Head shots

Your head shot is often the first contact a casting director has with you, so it is important that you make the right first impression. If the photo doesn't conform to industry standards, or projects an image that you can't live up to in person, you will seriously jeopardise your work opportunities.

ALL CHANGE!

A head shot (also called a 'ten-by-eight') should be a black and white 25 x 20 cm close up showing your face and hair and part of your shoulders. Every time you have a major change of appearance (especially hair colour and/or length), you must update your head shot, so choose your look carefully. You should change your head shot every five years or so, regardless.

The real you

The photo should look like you and express your personality and special qualities, or aspects you want to highlight, such as warmth, sensuality, love of the outdoors. It is not an idealised version of how you would like to look. If you've got a receding chin or a huge nose, don't hide these character features – they are the real and unique you. When you are called for a casting, if you don't look like your photo, you are wasting everybody's time and you will really annoy the casting director.

GOOD HEAD SHOT

The woman in the photo looks natural, relaxed and friendly. Her hair and eyes are lively and visible, and she is looking directly at the camera.

THREE OR FOUR YOUS

Don't try to look how you think 'an actor' should look. Look like you — a human being. During the photo shoot you can change your clothes and hair to present different aspects of your personality, so you'll have a choice of three or four variations of you. For instance, for commercial castings you need to appear very cheerful and positive, or you might choose a business look or a sexy look for specific roles, but your main head shot will be more general and show you being relaxed and comfortable, looking your age.

BAD HEAD SHOT

This version of the shot is bad — it is not as if she is wearing sunglasses or a hat, or has a visible cigarette (obvious things to avoid) — but more of her torso is visible, highlighting inappropriate attire. The way she is holding her hair is unneccessary and suggestive.

WHAT CASTING DIRECTORS WANT

Less is more?

Most casting directors are busy, normal people with a job to do – finding the best person for the role. They are on your side and want you to do well, but poor performance from you can be just the excuse they need to whittle down a long list of actors. You've got to give your peak performance and show that you are easy to work with, professional, cooperative, can take direction and are both energetic and at ease. Again, don't expect your acting talent to do all the talking. Sell yourself by being personable, relaxed, self-confident and, above all, well prepared. Treat everyone in the room with respect, as the scruffy person in the corner could be the director.

Stay true

Be open, honest and positive about yourself. The casting director wants to see your personality, so don't answer questions with one-word answers or talk your way out of the job with too much irrelevant nonsense. Don't be apologetic or defensive about the way your career is heading right now, and don't try to put on an act to try to give what you think the casting director wants – they may be looking for you. Try to be yourself, and stop trying to second-guess or trying too hard to please. When it comes to the reading, take a strong line and give results rather than a work-in-progress. Taking decisions and being committed is better than being vague, especially when sight-reading or improvising.

BE PREPARED

The main turn-offs for casting directors are being poorly prepared, desperation, rudeness, negativity and hostility. When you haven't had an audition for three months it is hard to hide how desperately you want the job, but that's when you need to be at your strongest, respect yourself and your abilities and hide your insecurities. Listen carefully to instructions and, when you get feedback, accept it politely and work with it. Don't get all angst-ridden while you work — they don't want to know about your process or your creative struggle to find certain aspects of the character. Casting directors, especially for screen work, are looking for results rather than potential.

Comfortable with yourself

Be confident and relaxed. There's no point faking, or you'll come across as either arrogant or pushy. Nine times out of ten an average actor who is comfortable in his or her own skin will get the job over a better actor with poor social skills, unless he or she is one of a tiny minority of super-talented or super-commercial actors.

PIPING-HOT TALENT

In TV interviews the actor Ben Whishaw (*Perfume*, *Brideshead Revisited*) appears shy, introverted and socially awkward, but he also has the emotional vulnerability, talent and attention to detail that have made him one of the hottest young actors around. In interviews he is fascinating to watch, because he has the courage to pause and really take time to think rather than give glib answers. It was no accident that Trevor Nunn chose him to play Hamlet so early in his career, above hundreds of other young hopefuls. Real talent always gets discovered eventually, although only a handful of actors are that good so early — at drama school there are one or two in every year.

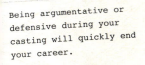

Being argumentative or defensive during your casting will quickly end your career.

A RISING STAR WITH THE RIGHT ATTITUDE

BEN WHISHAW WITH KAROLINE HERFURTH IN *PERFUME*, DIRECTED BY TOM TYKWER, 2006.

HOW TO GET TYPECAST

Young actors are often idealistic. They think they can play a wide range of parts (and they probably can), but in reality very few actors are given the opportunity to show the world their versatility. The smart ones recognise that they need to play to their strengths and present the image that makes them most commercial.

Uniquely you

Knowing what makes you uniquely you, as well as a recognisable type, is more exciting and rewarding than being an unemployed versatile actor. Most of the time, even in the theatre, you will be cast on how you *look* – and that is why the first stage of the casting process begins with sending out head shots.

THE BRITISH FOP

HUGH GRANT IN *NOTTING HILL*, DIRECTED BY ROGER MITCHELL, 1999
Grant is well-known for his roles as posh British nice guys – an image which has served him well in numerous movies and from which he is only now starting to branch away.

If you don't know what your face says about you, ask other people to tell you. If you are very self-aware or your type is obvious (eg, you are very attractive, or extraordinarily tall with a thug's face, etc.), then you can discover this just by looking honestly in the mirror. Ask friends — even complete strangers — to tell you how you come across, and what assumptions they made about you on first impressions, before they got to know you.

Get out of neutral

Like it or not, your face looks a certain way — it isn't a blank canvas from which to build a wide range of characters. If your face is characterless and average, and you don't fit easily into any type, change your appearance. Why strive to remain looking neutral and hard to cast? If this is your instinct, then it is wrong: your head shots will bear this out, rather than expressing character and getting you work.

If you are unique, and have an unusual style or distinguishable appearance, it can work in your favour when being typecast, although you have to be aware that this affects your versatility.

BE WANTED

You can find subtlety and versatility with every part you play, even within the same type. Once you become well known as a certain type you may struggle to break free, but who do you think has the better chance of convincing a director that they can play a part — a bankable actor with a recognisable face and 10 years' constant work, or an unknown actor who has had limited employment? Get yourself in demand and then think about exploring your versatility.

PREPARING FOR AUDITIONS

Before you start preparing for an audition, try to think of yourself as considering a part rather than hoping you get chosen. This subtle mind shift can have a positive effect on your confidence, making you feel like a proactive professional who is directing their career, rather than an actor desperate for employment. Research and rehearse as much as possible – you can never do too much preparation. Find material that is suitable for you and for the job and medium you are up for, prepare thoroughly and then present it boldly with commitment and confidence.

Choosing the right monologue

You should have at least four polished monologues ready to perform – preferably more – but you may also need to find something at short notice to land a specific role. Choose speeches that are contrasting in style and context, and characters that you could actually play and who are close to you in age. Monologues showcase your talent, but also demonstrate what kind of parts you would like to play (you may well be asked this during the interview, because the director might want to see how well you know yourself, and how intelligently you would cast yourself). The speech should last no more than two minutes; most directors will make up their mind within the first 60 seconds and then just wait for you to finish. You don't need much time to show off your talent – it's easy to spot very quickly how good an actor is.

A MODERN MONOLOGUE

DAVID CAVES AS JAKE IN *A LIE OF THE MIND*, BATTERSEA ARTS CENTRE, LONDON, 2006
Sam Shepard's play, written in 1985, has a fantastic modern male monologue which is perfect for an audition (although it is fast becoming overdone). The character of Jake, in Act 1 Scene 3, delivers an impassioned speech to try to justify the murder of his wife.

Avoid the big, well-known parts like Hamlet, Ophelia and Macbeth, or scenes that are difficult to communicate outside the context of a production, such as the climax to a play. Look for less well-known pieces, with a variety of emotions and thoughts that allow you to show aspects of character. Read the whole play, so you know the context and style. If you don't, you could misinterpret the thrust of the speech, as well as miss the mark with your characterisation.

Do the homework

Don't forget that a monologue is not a set piece, but the result of one thought following another, giving you the need to speak. Even though an audition is an artificial environment, you still need to find the thoughts spontaneously, as if you were thinking them for the first time. Read the script and find out as much as you can about the part you're going up for, the director and the company, and, if you have enough advance notice, go to see one of their recent productions.

Good monologues are often overdone, so try to find a few pieces that are less well-known.

THE THEATRE AUDITION

An audition is a job interview. That seems like an obvious thing to say, right? You want an acting job – that's why you show up at auditions. But you'd be surprised how many actors don't realise that an audition isn't just an opportunity for you to show what a fantastic, exciting, interesting, creative, edgy, fearless, technically brilliant and flexible actor you are. For sure, if you are poorly prepared or have an off day this will greatly sabotage your chance of nailing the job, but there's a whole lot more to a successful audition than wowing a casting director with your talent.

Think in depth about your audition and choice of monologue, making sure you do your background research so you know the context of the piece.

BUSY BODY

Keep busy, so even if you are 'resting' you can tell the director more than the names of the restaurants you've been working in. Don't volunteer that you've been out of work for eight months and that you are waiting tables. Keep involved in the acting world — keep going to the theatre and watch lots of films (expensive if you're broke, yes, but necessary if you want to keep learning, have opinions and find out about other people's work).

Auditions – a game of numbers

We'll take it as read that you have prepared yourself fully for the audition, but don't fall into the trap of expecting your acting alone to get you the job. There are many factors that are out of your control: often simply what you look like, what a director can imagine you playing (which may often be based on your previous experience and the kind of roles you've done before) and your status as an actor ('sorry, but we're looking for a "name"'). It's also a numbers game – the more auditions you get, the greater the chance that you'll land a job.

AVOID THE DRESS-UP BOX

Don't bring a bunch of props or hats, or whatever — you'll look like an amateur. If the casting call specifically asks for you to dress in a certain way, then do so. Otherwise, dress in a way that expresses your personality, but make an effort. You want to look like you, only better. If you've got a big personality or a cool grunge look going on, that's OK, so long as it is authentically you and expresses what you want to sell. You will be judged on your appearance, so be aware of what impression you make.

CAN YOU CUT IT?

A director or casting director wants to find someone to fill a role; sometimes they don't know what that is until they see it. All you should concentrate on is doing your best, being friendly, taking direction and being businesslike. (This doesn't mean turning up in a suit and being serious, but remembering at all times that acting is first and foremost a business.) They also want to know that you are a person they can work with, and that you have the personality, skills and professionalism to deal with the job.

The acting business

If you were attracted to acting because you hate 'business', then get real and learn some business skills – such as how to present yourself and build a rapport – as casting directors are only human beings. Casting calls can be the proverbial cattle market: you shuffle in, get photographed or filmed saying your name, and the whole thing is over in two minutes. But if you have a 10-minute audition, or a workshop audition, you can demonstrate your skills and make a connection. Face the possibility now that you're probably not as amazing as you think you are, so you'd better work really hard to improve your audition and people skills (the really talented ones are doing that right now).

THE SCREEN AUDITION

If you have been sent the script in advance, learn the lines so you can work without the script. If not, hold the script to the front and a little to the side. That way, it doesn't obscure your face and you also don't have to look too far down. Before you begin the scene, you will usually be asked to 'slate' – say your full name and your agent's name clearly to camera – and maybe 'profile' (turn to show your profile).

The person you are auditioning with can affect your performance, but if their level of energy is low or they are out of synch with you, it is important to maintain your focus — it may even work in your favour as the contrast between you becomes evident.

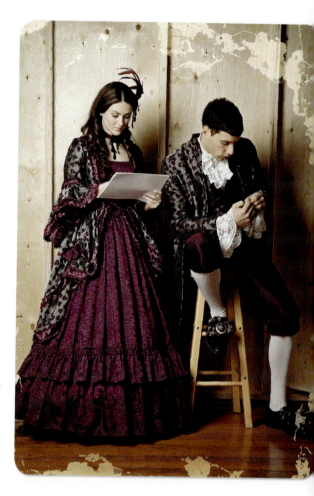

Brave character choices

Even if you've only seen the script 10 minutes earlier in the waiting room, make strong choices about how to play the scene (about character and what your character wants) and be committed to them. Don't be disheartened if you are asked to repeat the scene a different way. This is your chance to show that you can take direction and be flexible – it doesn't necessarily mean that your first attempt was all wrong. Directors like to direct, so listen carefully and take direction.

Other pointers

Assume that you are being shot in close up and scale your performance accordingly. The theatre credits on your CV show that you can act in long shot or medium close up, but if you have few screen credits, err on the side of intimate rather than theatrical. Don't overstay your welcome. When the casting director winds up the audition, thank everyone briefly and then make a confident and purposeful exit. Even after a good reading and interview, it's still possible to leave a bad impression with a clumsy closing.

KEEP YOUR PLACE

Find your cue so that, when the other person is reading in, you can concentrate on keeping your head up and your eyes alive, listening and reacting, rather than burying your face in the script. Read ahead so that you can keep your head up for the end of a thought, then look down for the next bit of speech. Keep moving your thumb down the page so that you don't lose your place. Use the punctuation to help you find the beats and show you where to breathe. If the other person is reading badly, or is giving you nothing, don't diminish your performance or fall down to their energy level. Support your reality and inner life by using your imagination even more.

Keep your face upright during an audition — even if you are not sure of the lines, it is best to look down every few lines rather than keep your head low as casters won't be able to see how you would work in the role.

COMMERCIALS

More than any other kind of audition, commercial castings want results, not potential. If they are casting a sharp businessman or shampoo scientist, then you need to dress for the part, and other aspects of your appearance – such as your hair – need to be fully formed (don't think 'I'll cut off my ponytail if I get the part', as your ponytail will lose you the job). The person who gets cast is often expected to deliver the same performance as in their audition because they will be so ideal. This means that you have to be the finished article. Don't save it for when you get the job.

Believability

Aside from looking right, believability is your most important attribute. Don't judge the material – the script may be bad and the lines corny, but you have to arrive at a fully formed performance within a moment, sell it and believe in it, and justify your words, actions and reactions. With all screen castings, make a decision and try it out – come with an idea and do it. They want to see results, not a work-in-progress. Even if it is wrong, it is better than making no decisions and going nowhere.

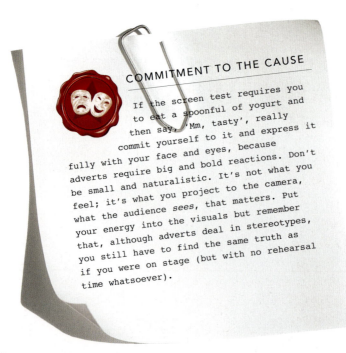

COMMITMENT TO THE CAUSE

If the screen test requires you to eat a spoonful of yogurt and then say, 'Mm, tasty', really commit yourself to it and express it fully with your face and eyes, because adverts require big and bold reactions. Don't be small and naturalistic. It's not what you feel; it's what you project to the camera, what the audience *sees*, that matters. Put your energy into the visuals but remember that, although adverts deal in stereotypes, you still have to find the same truth as if you were on stage (but with no rehearsal time whatsoever).

Commercial work is well paid compared to bit parts in films or TV. Some actors buy a house with the proceeds of a recurring ad campaign.

Commercials

Take a class in commercials acting. It will teach you details like how to hold a product without obscuring the label, and let you practise the mechanics such as slating, profile or reading off cue cards. It takes a lot of skill and quick thinking to act in commercials, where you've got to be able to make quick changes of direction. Watch lots of commercials and see how the actors conduct themselves and also what types of faces are used for different roles. Which ones could you be: housewife, police officer, scientist, tyre fitter?

10
CREATING YOUR OWN OPPORTUNITIES

This chapter explains how to promote yourself with a well-crafted letter, use the internet for casting, and create showcases for your talent instead of waiting for fame and fortune to knock. All areas of the profession are highly competitive, and should not be under-estimated, or viewed as a casual subsidiary to supplement your earnings. The one-person show, playwriting and scriptwriting, voiceovers and radio work are just some of the ways to broaden your opportunities, and they reward talent, discipline and top-drawer technique.

HOW TO WRITE A LETTER

During the early years of your career, and often beyond, writing letters to casting directors and theatre companies will be a major part of your job-seeking strategy, even if you have an agent. The targets of your self-promotion are busy people, and they will welcome any excuse to whittle down their slush pile of speculative submissions. A rash of spelling mistakes, the wrong tone or the whiff of desperation – however jaunty – can therefore be all the excuse they need.

THE RIGHT BALANCE

When you send a photo and CV, the covering letter must express your personality and attract attention above the hundreds of other hopefuls, but without being crass, gimmicky, clumsy, clichéd or unprofessional. This is harder than it sounds, as advertising — your letter — is a highly nuanced form of communication and presents many pitfalls.

The basics

Good old-fashioned spelling and grammar have always been important, so don't let yourself down with typos and shoddy sentence construction. How do you expect to convince the reader that you are an expert communicator on stage and screen when you can't even devise a competent sentence on paper? You don't have to have a degree to be an exciting actor, but you do need self-discipline and attention to detail. Poor presentation demonstrates that you lack both, especially when it's something obvious like 'William Shakspeare'. Unless your handwriting is exquisite (and legible), type your letter on a single sheet of white bond A4 paper and use a good-quality printer.

PERSONALISE

Though you may send out 50 letters in one go, each one must be personalised and addressed to a named person (spelt correctly) rather than 'Dear Sir/Madam' and, if you include a job title, make sure that it's correct. If possible, try to mention someone in the body of the letter that connects you both.

Even if there are no castings for them, send letters to theatre companies or directors you really respect. It is just good to get on their radar.

Clumsy phrasing

Your instinct for a succinct and well-crafted phrase will depend on your level of literacy; if you are unsure as a writer, ask someone who is more skilled to point out banal or hackneyed phrasing such as 'I am writing to yourself', 'I am an actor', 'I would be very grateful if' or even 'I am writing'. Another inadvisable but often-used phrase is 'I look forward to hearing from you', which is a veiled demand for a reply.

PERSONALITY, NOT EMOTION

Your letter can be chatty without being overfamiliar, and should express your personality rather than your mental state. Using subtle humour works, as does a very brief anecdote that gives the reader a glimpse into your life (this can also work as an icebreaker during an interview).

Attention-seeking

Very occasionally a truly original and well-timed gimmick may grab an employer's attention, but usually they are the first to reach the bin. Sending a complimentary bar of chocolate with your face on it, a humorous poem or tick-box questionnaire – or turning up uninvited with a pizza to share – will all be met with the exasperation and derision they deserve. A stylish and well-thought-out idea can, however, grab attention. On the whole, it's better to concentrate on being authentic and professional.

I'm really talented, give me a chance

Being an actor, you are probably a sincere and honest person with a strong desire to communicate and connect, but this should not tempt you to 'tell it how it is' and flout convention with your raw honesty. Don't say things like 'I'm a really hard worker and I'm passionate about acting', 'Just give me an audition and I promise you won't be disappointed' or 'I know I'd be perfect for this part' – even if they are true. Sophistication and restraint are preferable to emotional outpouring, no matter how heartfelt. Needless to say, any indication that you are desperate for work, or unhappy with your lot, will destroy your chances.

You must never show desperation (even if unemployment is eroding your sanity). You need to be interested and engaging.

FLATTERY

It is good to demonstrate an understanding of, and appreciation for, a director's previous work, but generalised flattery sounds dishonest and opportunistic. Avoid gushing praise, such as 'I love what your company is doing right now', 'I think you are one of the best directors working today' or 'I am dynamic and talented and would be the perfect fit for your groundbreaking ensemble.'

BUILDING UP RELATIONSHIPS

KARL MALDEN WITH DIRECTOR ELIA KAZAN, *BABY DOLL* SHOOT, 1956
Most directors have favourite actors they continue working with. Even if you don't get cast this time, the meeting is valuable.

Reveal, don't tell

There's no merit in pointing out that you are hard-working and a highly experienced team player. These qualities are taken as a given, and do nothing to sell you as an interesting and well-balanced individual. Rather than using a string of bland, empty adjectives, reveal a glimpse of your personality with a brief anecdote or stylish funny line. However, if you have specialist skills that are relevant to the job, by all means mention them in your letter (even though they appear on your CV).

KEEP IT BRIEF

Three or four paragraphs on one sheet of paper is sufficient. No one wants to read reams about your philosophy of drama, your personal life or your entire career to date — that's your CV's job.

SHOWCASE YOUR TALENT

In 1975 an athletically built, dark-haired Italian-American wrote, and starred in, a movie about an indomitable boxer, and went on to become one of Hollywood's highest-paid actors. When Vin Diesel couldn't get the roles he wanted, he directed and starred in his own short film, *Multi-Facial*; based on his performance, Steven Spielberg cast him in *Saving Private Ryan*. In showbusiness, you've got to hustle, because opportunities come to those who create vehicles for their talent rather than wait for the world to sit up and take notice.

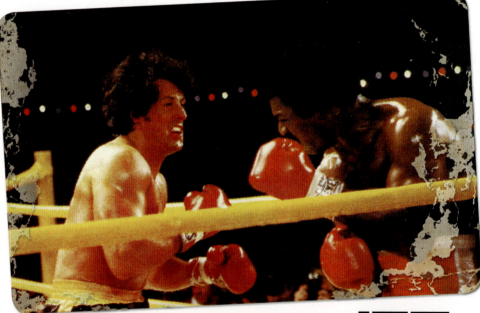

EYES AND MIND OPEN

You never know when a small opportunity will lead to a major break. The author of this book gained an audition for a cameo role in *Eyes Wide Shut* after Stanley Kubrick spotted him in a short film he'd completed five years earlier, solely for the screen experience and zero money. Furthermore, the directors of that movie have since won prestigious awards as mainstream independent film makers and screenwriters.

A PLOT MADE FOR ONE

SYLVESTER STALLONE IN *ROCKY*, DIRECTED BY JOHN G. AVILDSEN, 1976
Stallone wrote *Rocky* with strictly himself in mind for the lead. It has since become one of the most popular movie franchises of all time.

PLATFORM CHOICE

Whether you take part in an actual showcase (presenting a three-minute scene along with 30 other actors), a student film or a profit-share theatre production, don't expect to earn any money. The benefits are entirely artistic and publicity-related, so make sure you choose your material carefully.

Your showcase can be simple — a series of monologues without staging or props. The focus needs to be completely on you.

Hustle away

It is very tempting to stick exclusively with the temping or bar job and turn down showcase opportunities in favour of paying the bills, but hustling means taking calculated risks that may only reap benefits years later. It gives you something to talk about at your next audition, as well as much-needed confidence and experience. You can invite agents and casting directors to see your work as well (but don't expect them to venture too far outside their usual stomping ground – pick your venue carefully).

Showcase dos and don'ts

Don't: take part in a showcase full of bad actors with lacklustre direction. The parts are only as good as the sum, so you don't want to associate yourself with mediocrity.

Do: consider quitting if the production looks like it's going to be a turkey, but remember this is a contact-building exercise and it won't make you popular.

Don't: try to demonstrate your entire emotional range in one three-minute monologue.

Do: make sure that the showcase is well publicised and is in an accessible or prestigious venue.

Don't: drop out at the last minute to take paid work, unless the benefits dramatically outweigh the bad feeling and burnt bridges!

THE INTERNET

While some casting directors prefer to use hard-copy submissions of CVs and photographs, there are genuine casting opportunities online, including actor databases, and companies that send your details out to castings like an agent. In this fast-moving industry, the immediacy of the internet is a major benefit.

Casting directories

In the UK, Spotlight is the still the essential directory for professional actors, and is central to the casting process both online and through its hard-copy volumes. If you're not in Spotlight, you'll have little credibility as an actor, and only performers with recognised training or experience can join (for an annual fee). It has been online since 1997 (www.spotlight.com). Using a PIN, you can update your CV and have up to 15 additional photos, as well as showreels and voice clips. Casting breakdowns are sent out using Spotlight's free audition information service – The Spotlight Link. Other online casting directories in the UK include Castnet (www.castingnetwork.co.uk/actors/html/act_howtofindwork.html), which is for accredited drama school graduates only and costs a small amount per week, and Casting Call Pro (www.uk.castingcallpro.com), which has no restrictions and is free. There are also many online casting directories and resources in the US. These offer news and features, production listings, advice and online talent databases, so you can submit your media-enhanced CVs to an unlimited number of casting and job notices. You may even find a day job within the industry advertised on these sites: Backstage (www.backstage.com), the Hollywood Creative Directory (www.hcdonline.com), Acting Depot (www.actingdepot.com) and Casting Networks Inc. (www.castingnetworks.com).

In New Zealand and Australia, leading casting service Showcast is helpful (www.showcast.com.au). StarNow prizes itself on discovering hot new talent (www.starnow.com.au), and Mandy provides more international film and TV production resources than any other website (www.mandy.com).

Keep on top of your personal administration and check your email and phone messages regularly — no matter how busy you are, you can't afford to miss out on opportunities.

CREATE YOUR OWN WEBSITE

Being able to direct a contact towards your own expertly designed website can offer a more in-depth look at your abilities. Don't waste the effort unless you can create a slick site that is easy to navigate, which you are prepared to keep up to date. Make sure that your head shots are at least 300dpi so they can be downloaded and printed in reasonable resolution. Include CV, showreels, voiceovers and anything else that expresses your experience and personality, but keep it professional and don't make it so full of irrelevancies that it becomes an extension of your Facebook page.

> There's nobody else to come on and bail you out, that's for sure. It gets a little lonely backstage… It takes a lot out of you… because the energy has to go all evening without respite from other people. But on the other hand if you create something yourself,… that brings with it its exhilaration and its own rewards.
>
> Lynn Redgrave

ONE-PERSON SHOWS

The one-person show is a style of performance that has been with us for thousands of years, since epic tales, myths and legends were passed on orally from a single performer to the rest of their tribe. Many actors have created their own opportunities or followed subject areas about which they are passionate by writing and starring in their own one-person show.

It is vital to involve a good director, with a producer, for your one-person show. Directing yourself is notoriously difficult, no matter how clear your vision is.

What's their bag?

Christopher Plummer relaunched his Broadway career with his one-man show about John Barrymore. Simon Callow has toured the world with *The Mystery of Charles Dickens* and *There Reigns Love*, and Richard Dormer burned up the West End and off-Broadway with his multi-award-winning *Hurricane*. Lynn Redgrave won universal acclaim with her self-penned, one-woman show *Shakespeare for My Father*, and at the age of 70 Vanessa Redgrave won a Drama Desk Award for *The Year of Magical Thinking*. This is dramatic proof that even actors at the top of their game have to find their own vehicle.

NO HIDING!

The advantage of a one-person show is that you will have complete artistic control and can write to suit your talents and interests. However, you also have to work incredibly hard and be very self-reliant, with no other performers to keep you company. Collaborating with a good director is vital. You won't do your best work directing yourself, and you need a second eye to push you, to bounce ideas off of, and to… well, direct!

Performing in a one-person show is scary since all the pressure is on you alone, but all worthwhile challenges are daunting at first.

'I HAD BEEN TRYING TO WRITE A SCREENPLAY AND IT WAS GOING TO TAKE YEARS, AND WE REALISED IF WE DID A ONE-MAN SHOW, WE'D HAVE COMPLETE CONTROL.'

RICHARD DORMER

> The purpose of a screenplay is to tell the story so the audience wants to know what happens next, and to tell it in pictures. Movies are basically about plot. They're about the structure of incidents, one incident causing the next to happen. A play doesn't have to be that. It has to have a plot as some sort of spine, but the spine can be very simple: two guys waiting for Godot to show up.
>
> David Mamet

Take a course in writing to force you to start writing and to meet other writers.

PLAY- AND SCRIPTWRITING

Clearly here isn't the space to teach you how to be a writer, since whole degree programmes are dedicated to the pursuit. But it is mentioned as another way to broaden your scope within the industry, and to gain autonomy beyond acting. This section briefly compares the two disciplines of writing – for stage and for screen/TV – because many would-be writers find it hard to make a choice to suit their temperament and goals.

Stage or screen?

In theatre you can explore ideas; on screen you are slave to the plot (and the director, producers, studio executives, designers, production manager, etc). The balance between the spoken word and the visual lies on a spectrum, with plays usually lying at one end and screenplays at the other. In broad terms, plays rely more on words and ideas, whereas in film the audience perspective is primarily visual and plot-driven. So, while long dramatic speeches, big emotions and ideas may work in the theatre, on screen the impetus to progress the plot means that short scenes and quick-fire dialogue work well, and involves quick cuts between characters.

Shakespeare actually started acting as part of a troupe performing in the Globe Theatre in London. He only really found his forté when he became a playwright.

KEEP READING AND WRITING

Whichever path you choose, there is only one way to become a writer — write! Don't talk about how one day soon you'd like to do it. Start writing now: set aside time every day to write, and to read plays and screenplays. Keep going to the theatre. Keep writing. And don't give up until you've completed your first masterpiece. Then, be prepared to spend 10 years writing another nine masterpieces before you make your fortune!

> Professional voiceovers are the top athletes of the vocal world, and as such they are in regular training every day as they step in and out of studios on a regular basis... This doesn't mean to say that new voices don't turn up on the circuit – but it does explain why so few really make it – they've got to be very, very good.
>
> Jon Briggs

VOICEOVERS

Voiceover work has the refreshing benefit of having nothing whatsoever to do with the way you look. It relies solely on the quality of your voice and your ability to use it with imagination, versatility and technical expertise. However, competition is fierce (especially since lots of voiceover work is done by celebrities nowadays), so you need to have a top-drawer vocal product that companies will want to hire.

Complete control

The work is well paid – when you can get it – but unless you are already well known, a career in voiceover acting takes talent, discipline and complete technical and imaginative control of your vocals. There's so much more to it than having a 'nice voice'.

VOCAL VERSATILITY

Actors with deep, mellifluous voices have always been voiceover gold, but today there is more scope for 'normal' voices too. However, this doesn't mean 'average'. You need to have total expressive control of your voice as well as excellent timing, so that you can alter its timbre, tone, quality and pace to suit the requirements of the booking. For one job you might need to sound calm and authoritative and, for the next, be nervous and highly strung… or you might be a talking giraffe with a speech impediment.

Versatility is important when working as a voiceover artist, so being proficient with accents is a big plus.

WHAT'S GOING ON?

You'll need the quick thinking and vocal flexibility to switch tack in the middle of a sentence, sight-read a demanding piece of text at double speed, while maintaining crystal-clear articulation, *and* nail it down to 23 seconds… as well as sounding like the words are your own freshly minted thoughts rather than being read from a script.

VOICEOVER LEGEND

MEL BLANC 1908–89
Blanc was the voice of many Warner cartoon characters such as Bugs Bunny and Daffy Duck. He is widely regarded as one of the best voiceover artists ever.

JON BRIGGS

One of the most successful voiceover artists in the world is Jon Briggs (www. jonbriggs.com), whose voiceover demo page demonstrates a range of styles, and also classifies 'soft', 'medium' and 'strong'. Listen to his demos to face up to the colossal technical skill required. He also runs the Excellent Voice Company. If you are serious about voiceover work, you should download his detailed guide from www.excellentvoice.co.uk/advice_course.php.

Include 12 to 15 short clips. Place your strongest clips first and arrange the rest so that they contrast with each other. The entire demo need only last for a maximum of three minutes.

Demo DVD

Research the market exhaustively by listening to lots of voiceovers on the radio and TV, to understand what sells, and then figure out how to sell your own highly trained voice so that it grabs people's attention. Don't make a demo DVD until you have done lots of research and know exactly how you want to package your voice. If you send out a weak demo, you could spend years trying to repair your reputation. Send your completed demo to voiceover agencies – they will put you up for work if you are good enough to be put onto their books.

RADIO DRAMA

Radio drama is probably the most demanding and underestimated acting medium. In addition to having a flawless vocal and microphone technique, everything is conjured up in your imagination. The location, the spatial relationship between you and the other characters, the soundscape you interact within – all of it has to be supplied by you. On top of that, you bring all the homework that you would in a stage play (such as character wants, relationships, objectives and obstacles) ready to record.

RADIO STARDOM

HUMPHREY BOGART AND MAYO METHOT RECORD A RADIO PLAY, C.1940.

Be fully formed

Every radio script throws up a new challenge, and the pace of work is fast, as in films. There is little rehearsal, so you'll be expected to arrive at the studio with your performance fully formed. All the work of finding your character and experimenting with your thought processes and objectives takes place in advance at home.

IT'S HARD WORK!

In radio you will get to play parts that you would never be given in visual media because of your physical appearance or build. Also, you can fit it in between other work, and you don't have to learn the lines (although learning thoughts is just as labour-intensive). If you consider that between 75 and 90 per cent of human communication is non-verbal, clearly you have to work 10 times harder to get your message across on radio.

Radio acting can be quite liberating because of the lack of emphasis on appearance. Age can still affect the sound of your voice, but you are free of all visual constraints placed on the actor.

KNOW YOUR RADIO

If you want to be a radio performer, listen to lots and lots of radio drama. You'll learn about pacing, range and whether the silences are filled with thinking or just dead air time. You'll also learn about the structure of a radio drama and recognise the work of a range of producers and directors. If you can demonstrate a genuine knowledge and interest in radio drama and can talk knowledgeably about it during an audition, you will show that you approach radio as a serious art form rather than a way to supplement your income — there are no free rides in acting. Every area of the profession is competitive and demands technical excellence. Nowhere is this more true than radio.

WORKING AS AN EXTRA

There are a few benefits to working as an extra. You get free food (after everyone else has eaten) and the chance to experience the bustle of a film set and spot the occasional star. But it isn't a realistic path into proper screen acting, and it can actually harm your career if you become well-known among directors as 'just an extra'. A few months spent as an extra can be an interesting experience (if you like getting paid pocket money for sitting around all day), but you can earn more money waiting tables and further your career more by taking classes and hustling.

The extra's lot

Anyone can become an extra. Simply sign on with an extras agency, and be prepared to be called with minimal notice. A typical working day can be 14 hours long. You will be required at the studio or on location very early in the morning for costume, and will spend most of your time sitting around waiting for your few minutes of obscurity.

`Working as an extra is a good way to learn how TV and movie production really works.`

As a 'day extra', you will simply be a live body in the background, whereas a 'special extra' performs a special skill, such as juggling, riding a horse or playing a musical instrument. A 'silent bit extra' interacts with the principal actors in some way — maybe serves them a drink, opens a car door or cleans their shoes. Whatever you do, you're still just a piece of living scenery — there's no acting required. You'll still get paid, even if you aren't used, and if you use your downtime to run through audition speeches, read an acting book or teach yourself new skills, then your day won't have been totally wasted.

Extra dos and don'ts

Do: network with other extras and share information about agents and upcoming auditions.

Do: take advantage of the free food.

Don't: touch anything unless instructed.

Don't: offer to help out the techies – everything is union-regulated and you'll make yourself a nuisance.

Don't: pester the talent for autographs.

Do: watch how the professionals work (although most of the time you'll be made to sit somewhere else).

Don't: expect to further your acting career by being an extra.

Although you may get the chance to be on screen, you will be unlikely to get any lines unless you are very lucky, so get used to being in the background.

DON'T GIVE UP
THE DAY JOB

This final chapter explores the practicalities and realities of
self-employment and unemployment, and the world of rejection,
fill-in jobs and the struggle for personal fulfilment. It doesn't have
all the answers, but highlights the need to take stock from time
to time, sort your head out, assess your priorities and recognise
your achievements. The psychological demands of being a
jobbing actor require great resilience, and those who pull
through devise strategies to cope with its many ups and downs
and manage to turn adversity into adventure.

BEING SELF-EMPLOYED

Actors plus tax accounting isn't the best of fits – you didn't go into acting to become an expert in taxation. However, it pays to know about the mechanics of the tax code, your responsibilities and your entitlements, because in the long run it will reduce how much tax you pay, and stops you falling foul of the law.

Keeping organised and on top of your financial administration is vital when you are working on a freelance basis.

Keeping accounts

The best way to keep accounts is to use a computer program, such as Quicken® or Moneydance®, which you can use to track all your expenses, both domestic and business. Spending a few minutes every week keying in your debit card receipts and ATM withdrawals, and then reconciling it with your bank statement each month, will help you budget effectively. You'll never again be surprised by the state of your finances.

Deductible expenses

You can claim against tax expenses that are incurred in connection with your trade, business or profession. These must be 'ordinary' and 'necessary' and not be lavish or extravagant, and include travel (hotels and meals if overnight travel), vehicle and transport, equipment, clothes, newspapers, TV expenses, wardrobe, make-up, home office expenses, phone, legal and professional fees, computer software relevant to your business, DVDs and Blu-ray, concerts, shows, agent fees, promotional fees, haircuts, photographs, training and childcare costs. (See also Peter Jason Riley's *New Tax Guide for Writers, Artists, Performers and Other Creative People*.)

SEPARATE LIVES

For tax purposes, actors are classed as self-employed. The downside is that you need to keep accurate accounts and receipts of your income and expenses, and file a yearly tax return; the plus side is that, to reduce your tax liability, you can offset the cost of items that are incurred in the course of your acting business against your earnings. As a self-employed person it is your responsibility to pay your own tax and other contributions on your earnings. Even though you are a sole trader working for yourself, it's vital to keep your business affairs separate from your personal affairs, so open a bank account specifically for running your acting business.

Money matters need not be stressful if you set your accounts up correctly at the start — there are organisations and financial advisers who can help with this.

RESTING

It may seem incongruous that a book about being a professional actor should devote space to finding alternative employment, but it is part and parcel of being an actor, and regular work is a rarity for most of those without proven names. It's hard for actors to admit to themselves that they have to look for other work when the parts don't come in. But if you're really serious about acting, you will benefit from assessing and developing skills (such as typing or web design) and seeking out employment that pays the bills, is flexible enough to allow time off for auditions and is tolerable.

Waiting tables or bar work

It's the old cliché, but it has its benefits – namely, flexibility. You're also on your feet all day, which helps to maintain physical fitness of sorts, and you will also develop your people skills, since getting good tips is about being likable.

Teaching

From running drama classes to supply teaching or private tutoring, teaching is a popular second career among actors.

Teaching can be as creative and inspiring as working on the stage — but it is a large commitment which won't leave you any time for performing. A part-time option is best if you want to continue with your acting.

TEMPING

If you can type reasonably well, or have good computer skills, you can sign on with an office temping agency, who will find you a range of temporary work from general admin to receptionist. If you are organised, have good attention to detail and can learn new routines quickly, temping is better paid than waiting tables, plus you'll get to see the inside of a range of corporate environments. On the other hand, if you can drive a forklift truck or have other manual skills, there are temping agencies that cater to non-clerical work.

Retail

Its casual or part-time nature is a plus, and if you get work in a clothes shop you may also be able to get a discount on your wardrobe, which can be helpful for auditions. Also, you can observe people all day long (while you work, naturally).

Telesales

There are opportunities in sales and customer services. However, your pay may be heavily weighted towards commission, and you may be under a lot of pressure to make enough sales, or spend the whole day cold-calling customers and getting sworn at. Sales may teach you

more about how you project yourself to others, though, since you need sales skills for auditions.

Web design/ graphic design

A few years ago, to be a web designer you needed to know Dreamweaver or some other program, and before that, HTML code – it was a specialist skill. Today, it's much easier for amateurs to set up their own website than it used to be, but if you've been a hobbyist web designer for a few years you'll have better skills than most amateurs, and should consider making money from your technical knowhow. Take some classes to polish your skills and learn a bit about the industry. Build up a core group of clients that will give you most of your work. As long as you remain reliable and hit deadlines, you will maintain the flexibility to go to auditions, since you can work at any time of day.

Working as a freelance designer can provide an alternative income stream and leave time for your acting commitments.

WRITING

Writing isn't the closed shop it used to be. Good ideas always sell. If you have a good idea for a non-fiction title, sending off a proposal to publishers — a few paragraphs of introduction followed by a few sample spreads — can often be enough to get a commission, even if you don't have any previous experience. Fiction is more labour-intensive, however, since you'll need to write a synopsis and at least three chapters, and then the book itself will take several months to write — all for a similar advance as your hilarious bathroom joke book.

FIVE IMPORTANT QUESTIONS

If none of the employment ideas on the last few pages fire you up, ask yourself:

1 What skills do I have that I can turn into cash?
2 What new skills do I need to learn?
3 What training can I get to increase my employability and my income?
4 Do I want to work for myself or for others?
5 How flexible does my job need to be, and can I pick it up again whenever I need to?

(See also Lisa Mulcahy's *The Actor's Other Career Book: Using Your Chops to Survive and Thrive.*)

A MAN OF MANY TALENTS

ORSON WELLES 1915–85

Someone who was not afraid of trying everything, Welles acted in, directed, wrote and produced many films in his lifetime. Noted for his innovative dramatic productions as well as his distinctive voice and personality, he is widely acknowledged as being one of the most accomplished dramatic artists of the twentieth century.

GETTING PAID TO PERFORM

There are lots of ways to use your performance skills to earn money outside the usual waiting-tables-and-temping route. They have the advantage of keeping your performing instincts alive, as well as feeling closer to the industry than if you were working in an office. These two pages outline some common performance-related resting jobs.

Children's parties/ clowning

You may have to teach yourself some extra skills – such as magic tricks, balloon art, face-painting and telling jokes – but so long as you treat it with the same professionalism as you would approach any acting job, and you have some natural affinity with children (ie, don't do it if you can't stand them!), then you will test your skills as an actor, such as improvising and thinking on your feet. There are a few agencies dealing with children's party performers, but once you get your first few gigs you will get further work through word of mouth.

Circus is becoming increasingly popular. Take a course on the basics, and form a street-performing troupe.

CORPORATE ROLEPLAY

Many businesses, from multi-national companies to social services departments or the police, use actors in roleplay exercises to train their staff to interact with their clients or the general public. It's known as action learning. You will be given a character brief and then be expected to improvise and play for real. Interacting with non-actors while you are in character is a thrilling challenge that demands an extra depth of realism, not to mention nerves of steel.

PROMOTIONAL WORK

This can be anything, from dressing up in an Easter Bunny costume and skipping around giving out eggs and posing for photos, to giving demonstrations at trade fairs. Your acting skills are transferable to promotional work because it requires you to be creative, to think on your feet and often to learn a script or presentation. Dressing up in silly outfits? It doesn't sound too different from acting. The pay is good, because the work is often ad hoc, and if you are a team superviser the pay is even better. You need to be reasonably outgoing for promotional work, so if you're shy it will take you outside your comfort zone — which is a good enough reason to give it a try.

Murder evenings and weekends

If you are a good improviser and can think and adapt quickly, consider taking part in a murder mystery production. If you are willing to travel, you can enjoy a second income stream staging bumping-offs and ad-libbing with participants varying from partygoers to corporate team builders, and in a variety of venues. You may work from a script, or the whole thing may be based on a storyline around which you and the other company members must improvise. It can be very challenging and may really tax your brain, but it also hones your ability to engage, and hold, the attention of an audience. You'll also be working with other actors and flexing your acting muscles.

GETTING PAID TO PERFORM

DEALING WITH REJECTION

Rejection is an occupational hazard for all actors. They have to develop a thick skin to deal with rejection, while at the same time remaining emotionally open and available for their work. No amount of acting training can prepare you for the constant rejection, but it pays to sort out your attitude to rejection early on in your career – how you deal with it can make the difference between success and failure, not to mention the effect on your mental health.

It is natural to feel rejection keenly, but it is part of the career path you have chosen so it is important to become resilient.

In the audition loop

Remember that a casting director may reject you for one part, but keep you in mind for another. If you're driven and ambitious, like the salesmen in *Glengarry Glen Ross*, then you might think that you should be able to close on every good lead, but casting is not the same. Focus your energy on getting as many auditions as you can and working on your audition pieces, your skills and your interview technique, so that you are ready and prepared to take your chances when they come. Auditions are a numbers game, especially for screen work – the more you get, the more rejections you can get out of the way. So long as you're getting auditions, you are in the loop; it's when they dry up that you really need to re-evaluate.

A HEALTHY BALANCE

Focus on the future rather than the past. When you suffer a big rejection, feel it deeply (suppressed feelings will only cause you problems later on), then let it go and move on. Don't wallow in self-pity, because this will affect your motivation and hang around like a big cloud that you drag to your next audition. Develop a strong sense of identity independent of your work. Be passionate about acting, but find other interests and a healthy balance.

POBODY'S NERFECT

There are many reasons why you won't get a job, and it is rarely because of your lack of talent. You might be too tall for one part and too short for another; have the wrong colour eyes; or they may already have cast a tall, thin actor like you and want a short, fat person for the other role. A British actor/comedian was on the train travelling to the studio to shoot a lucrative supermarket commercial set in a pub, when the production company phoned him to say he couldn't be in it because he had just been spotted in a public information film set in a pub on TV the previous night. If you let them, incidents like these can send you crazy. You just have to accept that it's part of the rollercoaster, and sometimes it will work in your favour, not against.

Remaining positive in the face of adversity is not a luxury — it's a professional requirement.

PROFESSIONAL JEALOUSY

There will always be actors who get better work than you, and there will be plenty who would kill to have your career, or other aspects of your life. It is difficult to stop comparing yourself to your contemporaries (or maybe actors you've never even met), but asking, 'Why can't that be me?' is the quickest way to end up miserable. Does envying other people have *any* benefits whatsoever? Face it: there are no gains to being envious – it does nothing to help your career, but a lot to damage it. It makes you bitter, and erodes your confidence. Once you accept that it only harms you, you'll find it easier to stop indulging in it.

Jealousy can be used in a positive way to better yourself – but it is usually highly detrimental to your attitude.

'JEALOUSY IS ALL THE FUN YOU THINK THEY HAD.'

ERICA JONG

LIFE SWAP? NO WAY

The next thing to consider is that a person isn't just their career. You can't choose the best bits of someone's life and want them for yourself; you have to look at their whole life. Can you honestly say that you want to be that person and live their entire life – completely? Unlikely. If you do, then you have to have the mother who died when you were five, the broken heart aged 17, the car crash at 22... Get the picture? Live your own life and don't cherry-pick from other people's. Nobody gets to live the life they thought they would.

ACT ON ENVY

Don't ignore envy. If it eats you up and dominates your life, it's a sign that you need to make changes to make you happy, because happy people don't envy others. You can't really be jealous if you are actually happy with your life and, if you're not, find out why and make changes. And if that means quitting acting, maybe you should do that, too. Focus all your energy on making choices that are good for you, not envying the results of others — they may have made better choices than you (learn from their work and consider copying those choices), or maybe they just got lucky. It doesn't matter. Things in this business change in seconds, and you can always make choices, no matter how many obstacles get in your way.

SIBLING RIVALRY

OLIVIA DE HAVILLAND AND JOAN FONTAINE, C.1945
In a traditionally nepotistic industry, familial tension can cause rifts. The competition between actors De Havilland and Fontaine has become legendary in Hollywood, and resulted in a lifelong feud.

Never underestimate the power of jealousy and the power of envy to destroy.

Oliver Stone

> "You come out the other side, completely changed as a human being. I think I was happies when I was chasing my ambitions at the age of 20. I certainly wasn't happy when I achieved them. That's the price you pay for it. It took me years to adjust to that."
>
> Richard Dreyfuss

HOW TO BE A HAPPY ACTOR

During the course of your career, your happiness won't depend on where acting takes you, but whether it meets the needs of why you went into acting in the first place. If you want to be rich and famous, then you're obviously going to have a harder time being happy than if you love the process, the people, the environment, the unpredictability, the creativity and all those other qualities that being an actor offers you.

Embracing every aspect of your career with enthusiasm and pride will help every job become more enjoyable.

Global riches

You are able to think of pursuing an acting career because you're not one of the billion people on this planet living below the poverty line (living on less than $2 a day) or in a war zone. So you're a winner before you've even started – if you only earn enough to scrape by from acting, you're still in the top 10 per cent richest people in the world (check out www.globalrichlist.com)! If you are relying on acting to make you happy, then you are looking to other things aside from having your survival needs met.

Live for now

Some of the techniques used in this book are applicable to finding happiness, especially mindfulness – living in the moment. Instead of worrying about your audition next week, or the callback you are waiting for, concentrate on the here-and-

now. If you focus so intensely on one goal, so you don't have time for other things in your life, this will make you truly unhappy. You'll be a worse actor, as well. Be in the now, in the present, not just on stage but off stage too. That way you are living life to the full, not waiting for your life to start. Remember life is not a rehearsal, it's the real thing.

HAPPY FROM WITHIN

Once you are safe and have adequate food and drink, happiness only comes from within, from how you choose to view the world. Unless you learn to be self-reliantly happy, acting will never make you so, no matter how successful your career – you will either want more, or be scared that you will lose what you have.

The fear and excitement of opening night is still as vivid after 15 years in the business as it was when you first took to the stage at the start of your career.

'I'M JUST STARTING TO SCRATCH THE SURFACE OF WHAT REALLY MAKES ME HAPPY AND IT'S TAKEN ME A WHILE TO ADMIT THAT ACTING LIKE A LITTLE CHILD AND BEING A JERK AND A PUNK IS FUN.'

LEONARDO DI CAPRIO

GLOSSARY

General

A

Agent, theatrical: business person who represents actors in exchange for a small percentage of their professional employment earnings.

Alexander Technique: a movement technique which involves re-educating the mind to allow the body to perform with maximum efficiency (see pages 128–129).

Audition: reading from a given script for a play, commercial, voiceover, film, industrial film, etc.

B

Booking: a confirmed job in the industry; usually refers to print work, commercials, voiceovers, etc.

C

Call time: the time you are expected to be at rehearsals/ theatre studio/location.

Callback: second (or more) audition for a play, a commercial, TV, film, etc.

Casting director: person in charge of screening actors and selecting appropriate people to audition; works closely with the director to cast the show.

Composite: a group of photos on a single page showing a variety of poses, characters and/or expressions.

Conflict, dramatic: inherent struggle between characters, or within a single character, representing two opposing sides or views.

CV: one-page listing of actor's experience attached to the back of 25 x 20 cm head shot.

D

Diaphragm: the most efficient muscle for breathing, the diaphragm is an important part of the body for the actor, as instead of shallowly breathing from the lungs, a deeper, healthier and supported breathing is created – helping the upper body to relax, and expanding the responsiveness of the voice.

Director: the person who makes choices about theme and concept for the entire show/production, and who orchestrates the actors to achieve a desired result. Directors work closely with all designers and (in a musical) with the choreographer and musical director.

Dress rehearsal: rehearsal in which costumes are worn; also simply called 'Dress'. FULL DRESS includes all costumes and make-up; TECH-DRESS includes costumes, lights and sound; FULL-TECH-DRESS includes all costumes, make-up, lights and sound; FINAL DRESS is the last before opening; INVITED DRESS has an invited (non-paying) audience.

E

Endowment: an acting technique, endowment refers to giving objects used in acting precise physical qualities.

Exercises Plastiques, les: a series of challenging physical isolations developed by Jerzy Grotowski (see pages 144–147).

F

Feldenkrais method: a series of quiet exploratory movements that allow the brain to learn new skills in the quality of movement and exploration (see pages 138–139).

G

General audition: auditions prepared in advance by the actor, always memorised and blocked, usually monologues; audition to show ability; as opposed to a specific audition for a piece.

Green room: common room for backstage actors and crew.

I

Improvisation: used in the rehearsal process to free the mind, body, and stimulate ideas and physicality in a performance.

L

Laban movement theory: a system of studying the mechanics of human movement devised by Rudolf Laban (see pages 130–133).

M

Method, the: a set of repeatable techniques and tools to help actors draw upon their own life experiences to find realism. Developed in the early twentieth century in Russia by Stanislavski (see pages 36–41).

O

Objectives: the major wants of the character an actor plays.

Obstacles: characters always have obstacles which obstruct their objectives. The actor uses these to help pursue objectives with a sense of urgency or immediacy.

Off book: having lines memorised and able to perform without script in hand.

P

Pace: individual rhythm of the character; picking up pace means 'go faster'.

Period: the timeframe in which a production is set, established by the author or the director.

Portfolio: model's book containing examples (tear sheets) of previous work and photographs exhibiting potential.

Principal: actor category designating a role of significance, usually with lines but not necessarily; each union may define 'principal' in a slightly different way.

Properties: all movable things on stage; abbreviated as props.

S

'Semi-supine' position: a position from yoga practice which helps with relaxation and

breathing exercises – one lies with their back on the floor and the feet on the ground.

Showcase: a performance with the aim of 'showcasing' the talent of the actors, organised by the actors themselves and ideally with an audience including agents.

Substitution: a technique in acting in which people or objects are emotionally replaced with those from the actor's own life, for a real identification of feeling.

T

Talent: in film and television, the actors (as opposed to the crew) are often called the talent.

Screen

A

Assistant director (AD): in film, ADs perform functions of theatre stage managers: keep track of actors, call them in for work, act as a spokesperson for the director, etc. If more than one called 'first AD', 'second AD' etc.

Avail days: date(s) actor must be available for the shoot.

C

Cameo: a relatively small but highly visible role.

Camera left: appearing on camera to the left of the screen; to adjust camera left, move to your right.

Camera right: appearing on camera to the right of the screen; to adjust to camera right, move to your left.

Conflict, product: having a current commercial promoting the same type of product, therefore unable to accept commercial employment in that area.

D

Demo reel: film or videotape demonstrating actor's on-camera capabilities.

Demo tape: audio tape demonstrating actor's voiceover capabilities.

E

Extra: union designation for talent working on-camera but not in a principal role; also called 'background talent'.

O

Off-camera: work not appearing on film or tape, also called voiceover.

On-camera: appearing in film or tape.

S

Screen test: on-camera audition for film or TV job.

Squawk box: intercom that goes from the stage into the dressing rooms and green room, allowing actors to hear the show and follow its progress; also called 'monitor'.

Slate: to identify yourself by name at on-camera auditions.

Stand-in: the person hired to stand in for a star or principal player while lights and background are set; stand-ins do not appear on camera.

V

Voiceover: work in which the actor does not appear on camera, but the voice accompanies film or tape, as in a commercial or an industrial film.

W

Wrap: in film, and TV, word signifying the end of the job; professional actors may not leave a job or location until they are officially 'wrapped'.

Stage

A

Alexandrine: a line of verse having six feet (twelve beats).

Arena stage: stage surrounded on all sides by audience; also 'theatre in the round'.

Artistic director (AD): person who oversees all the artistic decisions in a repertory theatre or stock company; influential in selecting plays for the season, hiring the directors and resident actors.

Assistant director (AD): in theatre the person who assists the director. If more than one called 'first AD', 'second AD', etc.

Assistant stage manager (ASM): assistant to the stage manager. If more than one called 'first ASM', 'second ASM', etc.

B

Backstage: area encompassing 1) all the dressing rooms and common rooms for actors in a theatre production and 2) all the area immediately behind the set not visible to the audience, also called 'off-stage' or 'in the wings'.

Bio: an actor's condensed biography, used in a theatre programme.

Bit: in blocking, a small piece of on-stage business.

Blocking: the physical movement of all actors.

Book: in musical theatre, the sections that are spoken are known collectively as the book.

Box office manager: person in charge of ticket sales in the theatre.

Breaking the fourth wall: delivering a line of speech directly to the audience (see pages 72–73).

Business: in blocking, a small piece of physical acting on stage, often related to props.

C

Comp: abbreviation of complimentary ticket.

Countering: in blocking, counter-crossing, ie, moving in an opposite direction from another actor in order to balance the stage picture.

Cue-to-cue: a rehearsal that only focuses on entrances and exits and light and sound cues, skipping most of the acting and the play.

D

Down stage: the front of the stage.

E

Elision: in verse, contraction of two syllables into one, for example, heav'n.

Exeunt: Latin plural of exit 'they go out'.

F

Feminine ending: verse line considered regular but having an extra (eleventh) unstressed syllable at the end.

Foot: an iamb, composed of an unstressed syllable followed by a stressed syllable.

I

Iambic pentameter: type of verse made up of five iambs (feet), each composed of an unstressed syllable followed by a stressed syllable.

M

Master script: copy of the play marked by the stage manager with all the blocking and cues; used to run the show.

O

Off-stage: 1) backstage immediately behind the set and not visible to the audience, also called 'the wings'. 2) Heard but not seen, as in 'off-stage noises'.

S

Stage left: to the left of the actor as he/she faces the audience.

Stage manager: person who oversees the whole running of the performance and works closely with the director; attends all rehearsals and keeps the master script.

Stand-by: the person prepared to go on in a role if another actor is unable to appear; as opposed to understudy, the stand-by does not otherwise appear in the show.

T

Taking stage: 1) physical and emotional 'set-up' when the actor prepares to begin on stage, 2) dominating and/or using the entire stage, as in a long monologue.

Thrust stage: a stage surrounded on three sides by audience.

U

Understudy: person to go on in a (usually) larger role if another actor is unable to appear; as opposed to stand-by, understudy performs in another role in the show, but the stand-by does not. Also called 'cover', as in 'I'm covering (or cover for) the two female leads.'

Upstage: the back of the stage. Also, to draw audience focus away from other actors at an inappropriate moment.

W

Wings: immediate backstage, spaces to the right and left of the stage.

INDEX
Figures in italics
indicate captions.

ACKNOWLEDGEMENTS

Special thanks to Tony Bell for providing intelligent and enthusiastic feedback and his 'glass half full' perspective, my editor Martha Burley for her endless patience, efficiency and professionalism, and my beautiful wife Allison for everything else!

All interview quotes in this book have been collated from a variety of sources. Quintet has made every effort to avoid misquotations, but would be happy to correct any issues on future reprints.

PICTURE CREDITS

All other images are the copyright of Quintet Publishing Ltd. While every effort has been made to credit contributors, Quintet Publishing would like to apologise should there have been any omissions or errors – and would be pleased to make the appropriate correction for future editions of the book.

Alamy: 6 © Christopher Franko / Alamy; 7 B © Photos 12 / Alamy; 8 © Photos 12 / Alamy; 9 © Jeff Morgan 06 / Alamy; 19 © BlueMoon Stock / Alamy; 20 © Photos 12 / Alamy; 21 © Photos 12 / Alamy; 22 © Photos 12 / Alamy; 27 © Pictorial Press Ltd / Alamy; 32 © RIA Novosti / Alamy; 36 © Lebrecht Music and Arts Photo Library / Alamy; 37 © Lebrecht Music and Arts Photo Library / Alamy; 38 © Photos 12 / Alamy; 39 © United Archives GmbH / Alamy; 40 © culliganphoto / Alamy; 41 © Pictorial Press Ltd / Alamy; 49 © Geraint Lewis / Alamy; 54 © aberCPC / Alamy; 59 © Geraint Lewis / Alamy; 60 © Geraint Lewis / Alamy; 62 © Photos 12 / Alamy; 67 T © United Archives GmbH / Alamy; 67 B © Photos 12 / Alamy; 69 © Photos 12 / Alamy; 72 © Paul Wood / Alamy; 77 © Pictorial Press Ltd / Alamy; 79 © Jim West / Alamy; 81 © Mary Evans Picture Library / Alamy; 82 © Photos 12 / Alamy; 83 © Photos 12 / Alamy; 87 © keith morris / Alamy; 93 © Geraint Lewis / Alamy; 94 © Jack Carey / Alamy; 111 © Photos 12 / Alamy; 112 © Tracey Fahy / Alamy; 130 © Bildarchiv Monheim GmbH / Alamy; 132 © Lebrecht Music and Arts Photo Library / Alamy; 135 © Photos 12 / Alamy; 136 © Photos 12 / Alamy; 138 © Libby Welch / Alamy; 139 © Photos 12 / Alamy; 140 © Pictorial Press Ltd / Alamy; 142 T © Penny Boyd / Alamy; 145 © Coaster / Alamy; 151 © United Archives GmbH / Alamy; 155 © Pictorial Press Ltd / Alamy; 156 © Photos 12 / Alamy; 161 © Trinity Mirror / Mirrorpix / Alamy; 167 © keith morris / Alamy; 168 © Photos 12 / Alamy; 172 © Oliver Knight / Alamy; 175 © Mary Evans Picture Library / Alamy; 177 © Photos 12 / Alamy; 181 © Photos 12 / Alamy; 183 © Pictorial Press Ltd / Alamy; 184 © United Archives GmbH / Alamy; 187 T-L © Pictorial Press Ltd / Alamy; 193 © Mary Evans Picture Library / Alamy; 199 © Photos 12 / Alamy; 200 © Photos 12 / Alamy; 202 © Lebrecht Music and Arts Photo Library / Alamy; 215 © INTERFOTO / Alamy; 216 © Pictorial Press Ltd / Alamy; 221 © moodboard / Alamy; 226 © Pictorial Press Ltd / Alamy; 228 © Pictorial Press Ltd / Alamy; 235 © Image Source / Alamy; 236 © Photos 12 / Alamy; 239 © Mary Evans Picture Library / Alamy; 241 © Jimmy Lopes / Alamy.

Getty: 144 © Keystone/Getty Images; 244 © Silver Screen Collection/Getty Images.

istock: 16 © Joan Vicent Cantó Roig; 31 © Eduardo Luzzatti Buyé; 50 © Nathan Jones; 55 © Arman Zhenikeyev; 56 © Anna Bryukhanova; 100 © Mark Strozier; 104 © Kristen Johansen; 116 © Chris Schmidt; 117 © CAP53; 126 © Keith Binns; 141 © airportrait; 146 © Elena Korenbaum; 150 © Nathan Jones; 158 © Alf Ertsland; 159 © Gregor Hocevar; 160 © Bart Sadowski; 162 © Nathan Jones; 165 T-R © Nathan Jones: 165 T-C © Nathan Jones; 165 B-C © Nathan Jones; 165 B-R © Nathan Jones; 178 © Nathan Jones; 191 T © Chris Schmidt; 191 B © Chris Schmidt; 192 © Chris Schmidt; 201 © Nuno Silva; 206 © Nuno Silva; 218 © Alexey Khlobystov; 227 © Chris Schmidt; 230 © Kevin Russ; 237 © Christine Kublanski; 240 © jane.

Shutterstock: 12 B-R © Valentin Agapov; 13 B-R © JustASC; 14 B-R © Rodolfo Arpia; 15 C-L © Valentin Agapov; 18 © coka; 26 © Tracy Whiteside; 30 © Cindy Hughes; 34 © Alex Hinds; 44 © ChipPix; 47 T-R © Ragne Kabanova; 47 B-L © paul Prescott; 47 B-C © Viktor Borovskikh; 47 B-R © Teresa Kasprzycka; 48 © John Spence; 58 © Hank Frentz; 71 © Richard Upshur; 78 © Bairachnyi Dmitry; 88 © Complete Gallery; 95 © RTimages; 98 © Michelangelo Gratton; 108 © doglikehorse; 114 © Mihail Zheleznyak; 115 © iofoto; 121 © FXQuadro; 123 © Piotr Marcinski; 124 © YI CHEN; 131 © Edyta Pawlowska; 134 © HannaMonika; 137 © joyfull; 142 B © Lucian Coman; 153 © Dario Diament; 157 T-R © Jim Feliciano; 157 C © Kenneth Sponsler; 157 B-L © Kenneth Sponsler; 164 © James Steidl; 176© Diego Cervo; 182 © April Cat; 187 B-R © Korionov; 194 © Sean De Burca; 196 © Andre Blais; 197 © Andre Blais; 212 © Dario Sabljak; 217 © Ferenc Szelepcsenyi; 223 © c.; 224 © tonyz20; 231 © vgstudio; 238 © Leah-Anne Thompson; © Fnsy; 247 © Yuganov Konstantin.